Robert G. Wade

Playing Chess

BASED ON THE ATV SERIES 'CHECKMATE'

B. T. Batsford Ltd/TVTimes

First Published 1974
©Robert G. Wade

ISBN 0 7134 2895 3

Printed by Butler & Tanner, Frome, Somerset.
for the publishers B. T. Batsford, 4 Fitzhardinge Street W.1.

Preface

This work is based on the ATV series *Checkmate* which is being presented by television's famous magician and chess enthusiast, David Nixon, and was script-written by the author of this book.

The L-player is shown how the pieces move in such a way that, it is hoped, he or she will acquire an understanding of their power. The tactics of the chessboard are systemically presented in such a way that the reader may have a sample of every possibility stored at the ready in the memories bank. I hope that some of the essentials of the struggles for one's pieces to dominate the board will be conveyed from the chapter on positional play.

I am slowly beginning to develop the results of my experience from nearly 30 years of international participation on the human and practical sides of chess thinking and present an inkling of these in chapter 4.

It is intended that the television series should cater for learners and players of every category. Therefore I hope there is something in this volume for everyone. I found that I had misconceptions on many aspects of chess history before I started the work and have personally learnt much from doing this.

Besides the debt I owe to David Nixon and to Malcolm Taylor, the director of the Checkmate series I want to acknowledge my thanks for help in presenting this book from Peter Kemmis Betty, Costa Georgopoulos, Hilary Thomas, Tim Harding, Les Blackstock and Tony Hosking.

Roger Bridges, asked at short notice, to provide some sketches, produced a wonderful assortment of originals—our selection does not do him justice.

Kevin O'Connell, besides being most helpful in a general sense, took over the responsibility and carried out most efficiently the provision of many of the photographs. I am grateful to Freddy Reilly of the British Chess Magazine, Trevor Stowe of The Chess Centre, the curators of the Mansell Collection, of the British Museum and of the Science Museum, Peter Morrish, W. H. Cozens, B. H. Wood of Chess (Sutton Coldfield) Ltd., John Jaques Snr. of Jaques and Son, Burt Hochberg of Chess Life (USA) and the Novosti Press for their particular help in this direction.

Robert G. Wade

Contents

1 The moves and their history

Chess, as we know it, is about five hundred years old. The present moves of the chessmen have remained about the same since the mid-1500s.

But chess itself is much older. We don't know exactly when civilisations began to substitute war games and board games and armchair strategists for war itself. There is evidence that the 8 by 8 board was in use even before the Romans came to Britain, though for what games it is not certain. The chessboard of 64 squares and its two chess armies was in use in the Sanskrit areas of Indo-Pakistan about AD 550. Its aim then, as it is today, was to capture the opposing king. It is this singular objective that distinguishes chess from other games.

In Sanskrit chess the pieces may have represented the four arms of war—the chariot, the elephant, the horseman and the foot-soldier—plus a king and minister. Today the corresponding names are rook, bishop, knight and pawn, together with king and queen.

We know something about the four-handed game of Chaturanga—played around AD 600—in which dice were thrown. That a dice has six sides and chess six differing pieces may be no coincidence. If you threw one you moved the pawn. Two meant the horseman could move. Three—the elephant, and so on. . . .

Chess came to Europe in three ways. From Northern India it was passed on to Persia—it has been suggested as a gift between kings. Possibly it was taken back to the Caliphates of Baghdad by Arab traders journeying to Persia, or by the Arab conquerors of Persia (AD 640–650). The Arabs, as they expanded west under the impetus of the Islamic faith, took it along North Africa and the Moors introduced the game into Spain. Independently the crusaders brought it back to Western Europe as they returned from the Holy Land. And the Mediterranean traders carried it via Asia Minor through the Balkans and the Greek Islands to Italy. It was in cities of Italy that chess underwent revolutionary changes in the late 1400s and first half of the 1500s. Only the rook and the knight moves of early chess survived intact. All the other pieces increased their scope.

Another European influence on the game is the change made from the pieces being the symbolic representations of the elements of an army to the trappings of a royal court. The elephant of India became a bishop to the British, *un fou* or court jester to the French, *ein laufer* meaning a runner or messenger to the Germans, and so on. . . . The term queen (or lady in other languages) is a European conception. It must show the greater outward importance of the woman in European councils! In older times and other lands this piece was the minister and had a more limited motion than the king.

There are two chess armies: one has dark-coloured chess men and the other light-shaded. We refer to the two sides as Black and White, but it's hard on the eyes to play for any length of time with such absolute contrasts. The same objection must apply to the squares on the board.

The Board

It is probably a surprise to most chessplayers to learn that the original boards were not chequered. The earliest may have been merely lines drawn on the ground; later the squares were divided by lines sewn on to cloth. The chequered board was not so necessary. Our rook (their chariot or boat) was the only far-ranging piece. Then, no other piece went further than two squares diagonally. The modern bishop and eye have to travel along complete diagonals, and that makes the alternate colouring of squares essential.

We moderns have added one rule to the laying out of the board: it must be placed between the players in such a way that the corner square nearest their right hands is a white one (diag. 1).

The Rooks

The rooks—their appearance makes you think of a castle—start on the corner squares (diag 2).

The rooks are the wingers of the chessboard; in old Sanskrit armies they were the chariots, mostly stationed on and racing down the flanks. In some countries where chariots were unknown, the piece was symbolised by other objects, such as a boat to the people of Bengal and the Slav tribes of the Volga/Don rivers, or a castle to the Italians of the Middle Ages. Scholars are divided on the origin of our word 'Rook'. One thought it was Old Persian for a chariot.

The Knights

Next to the rooks go the horsemen, the cavalry, the knights as we call them (diag 3).

The Bishops

The bishops, these are the ones with the split in the head. They go next to the knights (diag 4).

They were the elephants in the old-time armies, but to the fifteenth-century Europeans the elephants were almost mythical creatures. From the sketch of the Arabic piece you can trace the elephant's tusks. Does the split emanate from this?

The King and Queen

The two remaining squares on each back rank are for the king and queen.

The queen always starts on a square of her own colour. The white queen is placed on a white square and the black queen on a dark one (diag 5).

The kings take the remaining squares (diag 6).

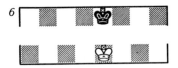

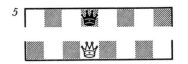

Checkmate

Though not as powerful a piece as the queen, the king is the most important. If he is attacked and cannot escape capture he is said to be checkmated. Then the game is, at once, lost.

The Pawns

Each side's eight pawns are stationed on the row of squares in front of their pieces. Our word 'pawn' is a corrupted form of the French word *pion* meaning foot-soldier (diag 7).

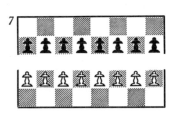

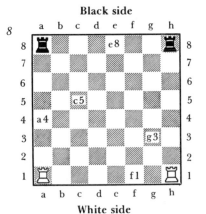

Black side

White side

Starting Position Summary

Re-checking where the pieces start—board's nearest right hand corner is a white square, rooks are put in the corners, knights next to them, then the bishops, queen is put on her own colour and the king has the remaining square; the pawns are lined up in front.

Naming the Squares

Each square is described by its co-ordinates, built up from the letters a to h

and the numbers 1 to 8, which diagram 8 illustrates. For instance the corner squares, on which the white rooks always begin, are a1 and h1, while the black rooks start from a8 and h8. The white army starts from the first and second ranks, and the black one on the seventh and eighth. In diagram 8 random squares are indicated.

The Moves—General

All the back rank pieces move forward or backwards; the pawns can only move forward.

Only a knight can jump over another chessman to a square beyond.

You are not to move to a square already occupied by one of your own men.

You capture by taking the opponent's piece off the board and moving your own man into its place.

Rook's Move

Rooks move to or take on any square along its file or rank. A **file** is a row of squares stretching between your opponent's and your own starting position; a **rank** is a row of squares from the left hand to the right hand side of the board. (In other words, ranks and files are at right angles to each other.)

A rook placed at a4 on an empty board can move along the file to a5, a6, a7, a8 or to a3, a2 and a1, or along the rank to b4, c4, d4, e4, f4, g4 and h4.

In diagram 9, the white rook at a4 can take the black rook at a7, but cannot

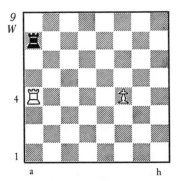

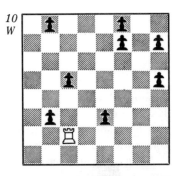

go to a8; and it cannot move to f4 (occupied by the white pawn) nor beyond it to g4 and h4.

Exercising the Rook As an exercise, take black pawns and place one on each of the following squares: b3, b8, c5, e3, f7, f8, h5, h7 and put a white rook on c2 (diag 10); with the black pawns not moving White is able to make eight consecutive moves with the rook, capturing a black pawn each move.

To do the exercise, cast your eyes along each square of the rank and file on which the rook stands. You are correct if you take the pawns at c5, h5, h7, f7, f8, b8, b3 and e3 in that order. Repeat this exercise until the action of looking along the ranks and files and making the captures comes quickly.

In the exercise in diagram 11 you are asked to name the square to which you would move the rook in order to attack the white king. Answer—to d8 square. This puts the white king in check. Check is a corruption of the Persian word *shah*, meaning king. It used to be good manners to warn the opponent when his king was attacked; but nowadays at international and club levels this courtesy is dispensed with. The less said, the better—that is the contemporary attitude.

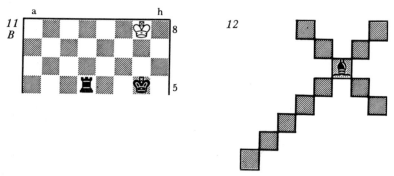

Bishop's Move

Bishops move to or take on any square along one of the diagonals upon which they are standing. Diagonals are the straight rows of squares of the same colour with corners touching.

A black bishop, placed on f6 on an open board, as in diagram 12, can move

to e7, d8, g7, h8, g5, h4, e5, d4, c3, b2 and a1 or take a white piece on one of these squares.

Exercising the Bishop (diag 13): put a black bishop on g7 and indicate which squares it would need to be moved to, in order to check (i.e. be on the same diagonal as) the white king on the following squares, 1) e1, 2) b8, 3) b6, 4) h4, 5) c1. Answers: 1) Bishop to c3, 2) B to e5, 3) Bd4, 4) Bf6 and 5) either Bb2 or Bh6.

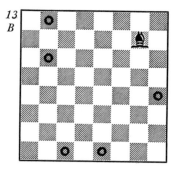
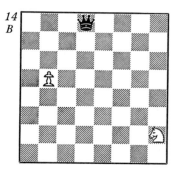

Queen's Move

The queen is the most powerful piece on the modern chessboard. It moves and makes captures exactly as the rooks or bishops do.

Exercising the Queen Put a black queen on d8, white knight on h2 and white pawn on b5 (diag 14). Find a square to play the queen to, which attacks both knight and pawn.

Answer: the queen can move to h8 and h4 to attack the knight down the file, to d2 to attack it along the rank, and to d6, c7 and b8 to attack it along the diagonal. The queen can attack the pawn from d5, g5, a5, b6, b8, e8, d7 and d3. The only coinciding square and correct answer is queen to b8 (Qd8–b8). With White having a pawn at b2 and a knight at g4 (diag 15), make one move with a black queen from f7 to attack both. Answer: Black queen goes to g7 (Qf7–g7).

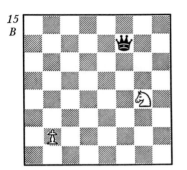

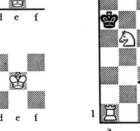

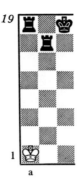

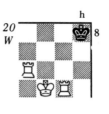

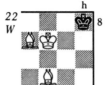

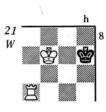

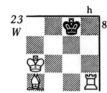

King's Move

The king is the side's most important piece despite its very limited mobility. It can move or take one square away either forward, backwards, sideways or diagonally. A king on e1 (diag 16) may be moved to d1, d2, e2, f2 and f1. A king on e5 (diag 17) could be moved to d4, d5, d6, e6, f6, f5, f4 and e4.

The King is Dead—Checkmate

To win the opponent's king is the objective of the game of chess. Indeed, if the king is checked, and there is no way its capture can be delayed or averted, it is said to be checkmated and game is immediately over.

The king must not remain in check on the move succeeding the one by which it was attacked.

Also the king must not be played on to a square where it could be captured.

The word checkmate is a centuries-slurred expression from the Persian language for *Shah manad*—the king is ambushed, and the Arabic word *mat*—dead. In fact the conception of checkmate seems to date back to Persian times. Before then the game ended with the physical capture of the king. The black king is in check to the white rook in diagram 18. One can consider three different ways of countering check. They are:

1) Take the checking piece. Here, the black bishop at c3 can take the white rook.
2) Interpose a third piece. The black bishop, when it is played to a5 shuts off the check.
3) Move the king out of check. The king can be played to b7, b6 or take the white knight at b5.

In diagram 19 the white king is checkmated. It is checked by the rook at a8. This cannot be captured. There's no interposition. The king cannot move to squares b1 or b2 as they are commanded by the other black rook. The game is over.

Find a move that checkmates the black king in each of diagram 20, 21, 22 and 23. Answers: 20)—rook to h6; 21)—rook to h5 (the black king cannot move to the squares g8, g7 or g6 covered by the white king); 22)—bishop to f6; 23)—rook to h8, where it is protected by the bishop.

Illegal Moves

If, after moving, you have left or put your king in check, or have made some other illegal move, the game is returned to the position before the illegality happened and a legal move is substituted; if possible, the move correcting the illegality will be made with the piece(s) first touched/taken at the time.

Knight's Move

The knight's move looks more complicated than it really is (diag 24). It has an L-shaped leap. It goes two squares along any file or rank, and then, as part of the same move, continues one square to the left or right. Diagrams 25, 26 and 27 give examples of its move.

9

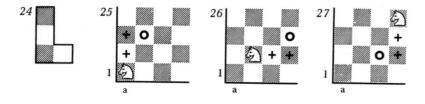

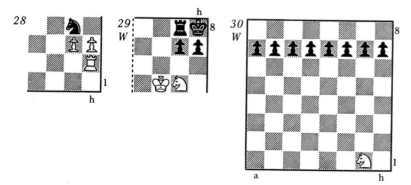

Moves Summarised

Ranks and files for the rooks, diagonals for the bishops, the queen moves like a rook or bishop, L-shaped leaps for the knight and one careful square for the king.

Pawn Moves

Each side starts with eight pawns lined up in front of the pieces. Mostly a pawn moves one square straight forward (diag 31). It cannot retreat. Each pawn can be moved either one or two squares (diag 32) ahead on its first move; the privilege of moving the pawn two squares dates back to the 1300s and 1400s—part of the Italians' impatience with the number of moves it took for the two chess armies to get to grips in olden chess.

Pawns do *not* take in the same direction as they move. Remember they represent the foot-soldiers of ancient armies; these soldiers would be guarded from frontal attack by their shields; when they met face to face, there would not be any obvious point of penetration. On the chessboard in such circumstances they stay put; in diagram 33 the white and black pawns cannot be moved. Their attacking stroke is the oblique jab forward round the side of the shield and this is symbolised in chess.

A pawn captures one square diagonally forward. In diagram 34 the pawn can take the knight; in diagram 35 the pawn can take the bishop but not the queen.

Like a good horseman, the knight is able to jump over obstacles. For instance in diagram 28, it jumps over g3, on to g2, turns and completes the move by taking the white rook at h2. An even more deadly example of its jumping ability is given in diagram 29; White can give mate by playing his knight to f7; all the black king's flight squares are occupied by Black's own pieces. We describe this type of finish as a smothered mate.

Practice for the Knight

The black pawns stay fixed on their squares throughout the next test (diag 30); the white knight is on its original square. White has 18 consecutive moves in which to capture all eight of Black's pawns.

Sample answer: The knight is played to f3, to g5, takes h7, back to g5, takes f7, to e5, takes d7, to c5, takes b7, to d6, to b5, takes a7, to b5, takes c7, to d5, takes e7, to f5 and finally, takes g7. Practise this until the knight's move comes smoothly.

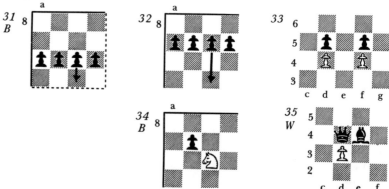

As a pawn cannot move back, what happens to it when it reaches the far row? There's promotion for it. It can be exchanged as part of its arrival move, for either a queen (usual), or a rook, bishop or knight. It does not matter if you have a queen on the board already; you can have a second; indeed you could have as many as nine queens on your side; in practice two should suffice. If you cannot find a second black queen in your set, use an upturned rook or two pawns on the same square or a lump of sugar or something that distinguishes the unit.

Pawn Move Recapped

A pawn moves forward one or two squares on its first move and one square thereafter; it captures one square diagonally forward; and at the far end it is promoted.

White Starts

In modern chess, the player with the white pieces always begins the game. For many reasons it is more convenient that one colour should always begin, e.g. easier recording and classification of important games.

Writing the Moves

The algebraic system using the letters a–h and figures 1–8 for naming the squares on the chessboard is the most widely used in the world. The descriptive notation, in which the squares are named according to the starting squares of pieces, is still common in English- and Spanish-speaking countries. This notation is described on p. 91. Both systems date back to about the eleventh century. But there is a steady switch from the descriptive to the algebraic systems in both the British Isles and Northern America. Most of the younger generation use the algebraic. From a publisher's point of view it is simpler and cheaper (perhaps as much as 25 per cent cheaper) to print. With paper costs soaring the inevitable change may have to be speeded up.

A move is a piece being played from one square to another. In writing the move in long fashion the same order is followed—piece symbol, square of departure, to (−) or takes (×), square of arrival.

Piece symbols are K for king, Q for queen, R for rook, B for bishop and N for knight; if there is no prefixing piece symbol, it's a pawn move.

The square co-ordinates (examples: a1, e4, g6) were described on p. 7 and shown on diagram 8.

Playing Through a Game

If White's first move in a game is pawn in front of king two squares, that pawn starts its move on e2 and finishes on e4; in long fashion that is written **1 e2–e4**. If Black replies with knight on g8 to f6 (attacking White's advanced pawn) that's written **1 . . . Ng8–f6**. When White defends by knight on b1 to c3 the score sheet would show **2 Nb1–c3**. Black's next move, pawn on d7 to d5—**2 . . . d7–d5**. White's third move is pawn on e4 takes on d5—**3 e4×d5**; Black's knight recaptures—**3 . . . Nf6×d5**; White plays bishop out attacking the knight again—**4 Bf1–c4**; Black's knight takes knight—

THE RED KNIGHTS

EVENT...... Baden-Baden, International Tournament...... DATE 25.4.1925

WHITE...... Réti ...... BLACK Alekhine

#	WHITE	BLACK	#	WHITE	BLACK
1	g2-g3	e7-e5	27	Nd4-f3	c6×b5
2	Ng1-f3	e5-e4	28	Qc4×b5	Nd5-c3
3	Nf3-d4	d7-d5	29	Qb5×b7	Qc7×b7
4	d2-d3	e4×d3	30	Nc5×b7	Nc3×e2+
5	Qd1×d3	Ng8-f6	31	Kg1-h2	Nf6-e4
6	Bf1-g2	Bf8-b4+	32	Rc1-c4	Ne4×f2
7	Bc1-d2	Bb4×d2+	33	Bh1-g2	Bg4-e6
8	Nb1×d2	O-O	34	Rc4-c2	Nf2-g4+
9	c2-c4	Nb8-a6	35	Kh2-h3	Ng4-e5+
10	c4×d5	Na6-b4	36	Kh3-h2	Re3×f3
11	Qd3-c4	Nb4×d5	37	Rd2×e2	Ne5-g4+
12	Nd2-b3	c7-c6	38	Kh2-h3	Ng4-e3+
13	O-O	Rf8-e8	39	Kh3-h2	Ne3×c2
14	Rf1-d1	Bc8-g4	40	Bg2×f3	Nc2-d4
15	Rd1-d2	Qd8-c8	41	Resigned	
16	Nb3-c5	Bg4-h3	42		
17	Bg2-f3	Bh3-g4	43		
18	Bf3-g2	Bg4-h3	44		
19	Bg2-f3	Bh3-g4	45		
20	Bf3-h1	h7-h5	46		
21	b2-b4	a7-a6	47		
22	Ra1-c1	h5-h4	48		
23	a2-a4	h4×g3	49		
24	h2×g3	Qc8-c7	50		
25	b4-h5	a6×b5	51		
26	a4×b5	Re8-e3	52		

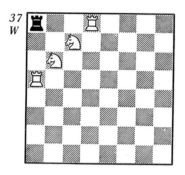

4 ... Nd5×c3; White does not take back, but brings his queen out— 5 Qd1-f3; Black tries to save his knight 5 ... Nc3-a4; White's queen takes a pawn near Black's king with check—6 Qf3×f7+ (+ for check); Black's king moves—6 ... Ke8-d7; White's queen checks at f5—7 Qf7-f5+; the black king is played to c6—7 ... Kd7-c6; White's queen checks at b5—8 Qf5-b5+; Black's king has one move—8 ... Kc6-d6; White's queen gives checkmate—9 Qb5-d5 mate (diag 36).

In the shorter form of the algebraic notation the game would be written **1 e4 Nf6 2 Nc3 d5 3 ed N×d5 4 Bc4 N×c3 5 Qf3 Na4?** (? by commentator for a weak move) **6 Q×f7+ Kd7 7 Qf5+ Kc6 8 Qb5+ Kd6 9 Qd5 mate.** Only the arrival square is mentioned. Some reference to the departure square would be made, if two different pieces could end up on the arrival square, e.g. from diagram 37, Ra5×a8 is shortened to Ra×a8 or R5×a8, and Nb6×a8 is written N6×a8 or Nb×a8. Note that White's 3rd move was written in short form as ed; this is decoded as White's pawn on the e-file takes something black on the d-file.

The Four Moves Checkmate Game

(The pieces are set up ready to start a game; the corner square nearest your right hand is white).

A conventional beginning. White plays **1 e2-e4**; it opens the door for the bishop and the queen to emerge. Black replies similarly: **1 ... e7-e5**.

White's second move brings the bishop into play: **2 Bf1-c4**, and Black copies with **2 ... Bf8-c5**.

Next White plays the queen out along the diagonal as far as it can go: **3 Qd1–h5**. It's bearing on three of Black's pawns, one in the centre unprotected, one next to the king only partially protected and the one in front of the black rook which is adequately guarded. Black replies **3 . . . d7–d6** (diag 38). He's seen the threat to his central pawn; he's missed the more important one.

White plays **4 Qh7 × f7** and announces checkmate. The queen is attacking the black king and cannot be taken by it—the king cannot move on to the diagonal of White's bishop at c4. White's queen covers also Black's three flight squares (f8, e7 and d7). It really is checkmate.

Chess games are lost through mistakes being made. What was Black's mistake? After **1 e4 e5 2 Bc4 Bc5 3 Qh5** Black can defend both the attacked points (e5 and f7) in his position by **3 . . . Qe7**.

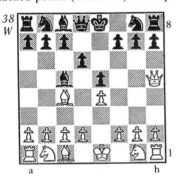

The Two Move Game

The next game shows the shortest possible road to checkmate. White starts **1 g2–g4**; that's not nearly as good as moving one of the central pawns (c, d, e or f); moving the g-pawn one square is safer. In my knowledge no first class game has ever opened with the edge pawns being played to a4, h4 or h3.

The game continues **1 . . . e7–e5!** (! means a good move) **2 f3??** (??= very bad move). This opens up a line of approach to White's king—along the diagonal e1–f2–g3–h4 (diag 39). Black can checkmate by **2 . . . Qd8–h4**. The white king cannot be moved off the diagonal and there's no piece placed so as to be interposed between it and the black queen nor to capture the queen. This particular game is bluntly named Fool's Mate.

Special Moves—Castling

(In giving rook and king moves earlier in this chapter I deliberately omitted the special move involving both these pieces in order that L-readers could get started on a game.)

Castling is carried out from diagram 40 by placing the king two squares along the back rank (Ke1–g1), and then placing the rook involved (in this case h1) over the king and on to the square next beyond (f1), both operations together counting as a single move. (Diag 41).

The castling move can be made either way along the rank—and in doing it the king is always played two squares, e.g. it's Ke8–c8 together with Ra8–d8 (diag 42).

In the form that I have described it, the castling move dates from the fifteenth/sixteenth centuries; it seems to be derived from a much older king's leap in which the king was allowed, once during a game, to make a knight's move.

There are five conditions attached to the modern castling move.
You cannot castle:
1 if the king has already moved during the game;
2 if the rook, being used, has already moved;
3 while the king is in check, as in diagram 43 to the bishop;
4 if the king has to cross over a square on which it could be taken. (Diagram 44 shows the white rook at f5 attacking the square f8—Black cannot castle yet)
5 while there is a piece on a square between the king and rook, as in diagram 45.

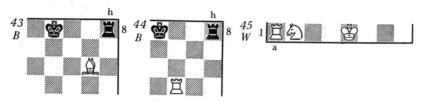

Re-capping: You can't castle if the king has moved, or with a rook that's moved, or while in check, or if the king jumps over a contested square, or if there is something between. Method is king two squares and rook over it to next door.

The special castling moves are written as **0–0** for castling on the short side (Ke1–g1/Ke8–g8) and **0–0–0** for castling on the long side (Ke1–c1/Ke8–c8).

Special Moves—Pawns taking En Passant

Pawn taking en passant or pawn taking in passing is the least known and most misunderstood operation in the laws of chess.

The initial double move for each pawn dates back to the 1400s, though it didn't become standardised until about the mid 1500s. During this time, it was found, there was a tendency for the two step move to lead to blocked pawn chains—something akin to the trench warfare of 1914–18. That didn't suit the dashing Italians, who invented the pawn taking pawn en passant capture. This ensured that when a pawn was moved two squares on its initial move it would not evade capture by an opponent's pawn on an adjacent file.

In diagram 46, if White pushes his pawn to b3 the black pawn at c4 can take it. If White plays the pawn at once two squares, the black pawn at c4 can still take it. The procedure is as follows: on the move succeeding 1 b2–b4 only, Black pushes the white pawn b4 back to b3 and, as part of the same move, captures it by 1 . . . c4 × b3.

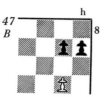

In diagram 47 Black plays 1 . . . h7–h5 and, on the very next move, White pushes the black pawn back to h6 and plays g5 × h6; Black can continue 2 . . . g7 × h6 and the game goes on.

Some Perspective

Now that a knowledge of the moves has been acquired one can set about building up experience by playing games. Before one can expect to beat Bobby Fischer for his world title there lies toil, success, disappointments and study. One can start augmenting one's experience by a study of the techniques and ideas of the masters—most of their important achievements in the recorded moves of their games.

Chess is not so much an intellectual pastime as, at its best, a tough unrelenting tussle which will draw upon the full physical, mental and nervous qualities of the individuals involved.

Basic Attacking Methods

As a further step on the chess ladder one can gain a knowledge of basic methods of attacking. The three games that have been included so far in this chapter have shown straightforward attacks directed against a single target—the king. Another effective form of attack occurs when a move can be directed against two targets—a double attack. It can arise in a variety of shapes.

There is the knight fork. The knight is checking the black king in diagram 48 and, at the same time, it is also attacking the rook.

The bishop on b5 is pinning the rook on d7 against the black king in diagram 49. It is illegal for the rook to move, as that would expose the black king to capture. It would also be a pin if the black king was replaced by a queen; Black could not afford to move the rook as the queen is much more valuable than the bishop.

To the housewife, a skewer was a wooden and later a metal rod pushed through old-fashioned roasts of beef to hold them in shape. To a chessplayer, a skewer is the action of the black rook in diagram 50 through the white king—which as the most important piece has to give way—leaving the knight in the rook's path.

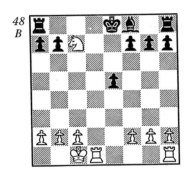

48
B

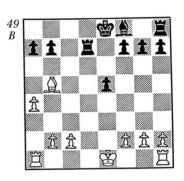

49
B

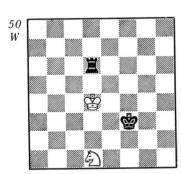

50
W

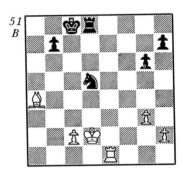

51
B

Value of pieces

Which piece is the most valuable to win?

Practically all one's pieces can be sacrificed if this leads to the opposing king being checkmated—diagram 52 illustrates an exotic example. White forces mate by **1 Qe3–h6+ Kg7×h6 2 h5×g6+ Kh6–g5 3 Rh1–h5+ Kg5×h5 4 f3–f4+ Nd4×e2 5 Nd5–f6+ Kh5–h6 6 Rb1–h1+ Kh6–g7 7 Nf6–e8+ Rf8×e8 8 Rh1×h7+** and **9 Rh7×f7** mate. White sacrificed queen, rook, bishop and knight. There are other tries for Black, e.g. 1 . . . Kh8 2 Q×h7+, 3 h5×g6++ (double check), 4 R×h7 mate; or 2 . . . Kg7 3 R×h7 mate; or 4 . . . K moves 5 Rh1+ and two more rook moves at most; 5 . . . Kh4 6 Rh1+ Qh3 6 R×h3 mate. Therefore it is not possible to give the king a price tag.

Any values assigned to the other pieces must be regarded as a rough guide. With pawn counting as a basic one unit,

Knight = 3 pawns
bishop = 3 pawns
rook = 5 pawns
queen = 9–10 pawns

These are not hard and fast values; obviously a pawn likely to become a

I want to draw your attention to the position, in diagram 51, of the white king at d2 in relation to the black rook at d8. Move the black knight at d5 anywhere and the white king is in check, a check which must be attended to—in the meantime what damage will the knight be inflicting? All such uncovering manoeuvres are termed discovered attacks, and, in this particular instance, a discovered check. What knight move would Black play? We would examine all eight squares to which the knight could be played—e3, f4, f6, e7, c7, c3, b4, b6; best seems **1 . . . Nd5–b6+ 2 K moves Nb6× a4** winning the bishop.

In all these preliminary examples of double attack, the king has been included as one of the targets. This is merely for emphasis; forks, pins, skewers and discovered attacks can involve any piece.

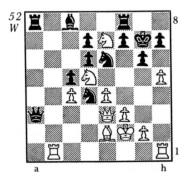

52
W

a   h

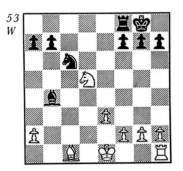

53
W

15

queen has a higher value. Bishops and knights are worth about $3\frac{1}{3}$ pawns early in the game and barely three in the endgame stages.

Parrying Attacks

A knowledge of defensive resources is important to both the attacking player who should reckon with them in his calculations as well as to the defender. We have seen (p. 9) and anew from diagram 53, that checks can be parried by:

1 capturing the checking piece (Nd5×b4)
2 moving off the line of attack (Ke1–e2)
3 interposing a piece (Bc1–d2).

These three ideas apply equally to the defence of situations other than check as in diagram 54 where the black queen (g4) is attacking the rook (d1). White can interpose queen (Qf3) or pawn (f2–f3), but of course the piece thrust into the gap should, if possible, not exceed the value of the attacker; if the attacking piece at g4 was a bishop (instead of the queen), it would be nonsense to interpose the queen. The rook can also be moved.

There are additional resources applicable against attacks other than checks; there is counter-attack against a target of greater or at least equal importance. Diagram 54 is also an example of this; instead of interposing, White can play **1 Qe3–e7** threatening to take the black rook and, at the same time, mate. This is a counter-attack. In return Black can rid himself of the attack by forcing a queen swap through the check **1 . . . Qg4–e4**; after **2 Qe7×e4 d5×e4** the skirmish has come to an end.

Game

White opened **1 f2–f4** which isn't popular, as it does not immediately help to bring a back ranker into play—bringing his king out is the very last thing White wants to do at this stage of the game. Black sacrificed a pawn by **1 . . . e7–e5 2 f4×e5 d7–d6 3 e5×d6 Bf8×d6** in order to make his queen and both bishops ready for action. White played **4 Nb1–c3** which is a good idea to the extent that it's an attempt to bring a piece into play. But it's the wrong move; his king's security problems are missed or ignored; if White had played the other knight (Ng1–f3) the coming disaster would have been

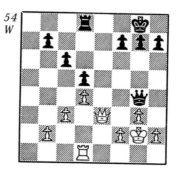

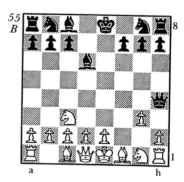

averted. Now Black finishes the game with a short violent attack by **4 . . . Qd8–h4+ 5 g2g3** (diag 55) this is the only way to meet the check, but the barrier is brushed aside by **5 . . . Bd6×g3+ 6 h2×g3 Qh4×g3** mate.

How to Win

There are three ways for you to win a chess game. You checkmate your opponent. He can resign the game as he sees that checkmate is inevitable, either in the short term or long run, and that you have the necessary experience or knowledge to carry out the winning plan. The third way occurs at expert levels, when you are using the special chess clocks and your opponent fails to make sufficient moves within the fixed time limit. (More about this on p. 23.) In the game, given in the last paragraph, the white player, if he had seen the cunning checkmate, could have resigned with honour and dignity or whatever he resigns with, after **4 . . . Qh4+**.

How do Draws Come About?

Fischer and Spassky, during their historic encounter in 1972, drew 11 of their 21 games. There are four ways of drawing.

The most usual is by agreement. One player asks 'Draw?' and the offer is accepted. The most common reason for this procedure is lack of a mating force left on the board. Two bare kings (diag 56)—hopeless draw. Neither a single bishop (diag 57) nor a lone knight (diag 58) can cover the adjacent square needed to construct a mating net.

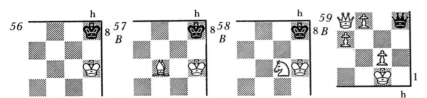

A substantiated claim, that the position has happened (or is about to happen) three times, with the same player to move each time, automatically terminates the game. There are many technical points about this particular rule, e.g. the positions need not occur on successive moves. . . . In case of difficulty you should obtain a copy of *The Laws of Chess* from your national chess federation or from Pitman Publishing. In diagram 59 the black queen keeps on checking by . . . **Qh4–e1** and . . . **Qe1–h4**.

A draw can also be claimed and conceded after both players have made 50 moves during which there has been no capture made nor pawn moved. If a pawn is played on move 49 you start counting all over again.

In both the repetition and 50 move rules, the draw can only be claimed by the player whose turn it is to move. You must not interrupt or distract your opponent during his thinking time.

Stalemate

The fourth and most intriguing way to make a draw is through stalemate. This arises when the player whose turn it is to move and whose king is *not* in check, has *no* move. In diagram 60, the black king is not in check, and cannot move on to squares covered by the white king (g7, f7 and e7) and the pawn (e8 and g8). Stalemate is the verdict in the queen endings (diags 61 and 62) if it is White to move.

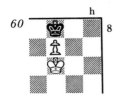
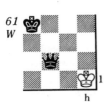
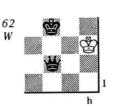

Pieces Active as a Team

What should one be trying to do early in the game? Mate the opponent if the opportunity arises. But there may be no weaknesses along the approaches to his king. Then you will need to battle for lesser advantages and achievements as a stepping stone towards victory.

As a preliminary towards building up an overwhelming array of forces in the vicinity of the enemy king, it's important to bring all your back row pieces into action; all that is, except the king, which must be kept out of harm's way.

Treat your pieces as a team. Place each of them where they are poised and active. Have them marking and restraining the opponent's.

Do not adventure with the queen alone. In the first games given, early forays with the queen brought success, but examine them carefully. In the first example (p. 12) the queen came out prematurely and White's victory was gained by Black's major mistake on his third move, in the second the queen's move gave mate, while in the third the attack with the queen was demonstrably decisive.

Have a look at Spassky's position (diag 63) from a game in the 1973 USSR Championship; he's White. His knights and bishops have left the back rank and taken up posts within reach of the black position; his queen is ready to sally further afield; the rooks are stationed on the threshold of the most open files; his king is castled. Spassky's position is nearly ideal; he felt ready to attack; turn to p. 43 to see how the game went.

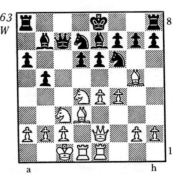

17

2 Sets and equipment

Chess sets come in a great variety of forms. Complete chess sets of the pieces used in the very first years of the game in India and Pakistan do not seem to exist. Those were the years when the rulers lived in circumstances of great power and pomp and one should expect sets may have been magnificently ornate in ivory to match the style of living. The British Museum has fragments of pieces found in the ruins of Mansura—about 50 miles NE of Hyderabad—which was destroyed by earthquake in the early 1000s. They were originally of ivory, but have deteriorated to a slightly chalky condition.

From before then, museums all over the world have the odd piece(s).

Arab Sets

Arab sets had to conform to the rigid laws of Islam—no graven image of animal or man. So a lot had to be left to the imagination. Even the sym-

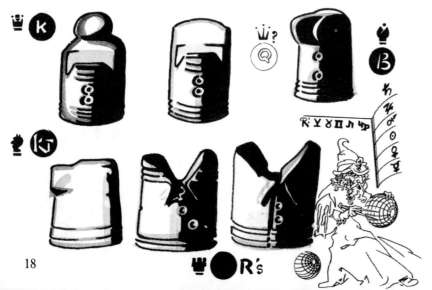

bolism adopted rarely satisfied the holy men. It may be possible to see a faint outline of the horse's features in the sketch. It is easy to see how the chariot or ship for the orient, so represented, had no trouble changing in Europe to a galleon, tower or castle. Probably Arab pieces were made from quartz or bone.

Chess arrived in Europe possibly as early as the 800s and as the centuries went by the faceless Arab pieces slowly changed.

The chess pieces found at Ager in Catalonia, Spain and the Charlemagne chessmen in the Dom, Osnabruck, West Germany still show the influence of the Arab pieces very strongly. H. J. R. Murray in his monumental work *A History of Chess* (Oxford University Press) describes early European conventional pieces '. . . the Kings and Queens were represented by figures shaped roughly as a throne, the Aufin (Old French for a bishop) and knight by cylindrical figures, the Aufin with two projecting lumps—possibly to represent the elephant's tusks, the knight with one lump to represent the horse's head, the Rook by a narrow rectangular block with a deep depression across the top, and the Pawn by a smaller thimble-shaped piece.'

In Europe the pieces began to represent the structure of society—something very much an issue of those times. The game of war was frowned upon. Something of the morality play was thrown into its composition.

The Lewis Pieces

The Lewis chess set (see photo) is based on 78 pieces that were found on the Isle of Lewis in 1831: 63 are now in the British Museum and 11 in the Scottish National Museum. A Lewis type queen was found independently in County Neath, Ireland, probably in the 1840s. Experts say they were made before AD 1200. The Lewis pieces are magnificently carved. The king has his broadsword. The horses under the knights are small, pony-like. Our castle of today seems to be represented by the guard; if you like simplicity

of lines you'll find it the most attractive; the plain shield; the sword at the ready. You can compare this set with the photo of the Leipzig set—it's a replica of one from the 13th century. Look at the ornate carving on the backs. It must have been made for a great king.

The chessmen illustrating the English edition of Cessolis' *The Game and Playe of the Chesse*, are shown next.

Chessmen from Caxton's "Game of Chess."

This is from the second book to be printed in the English language—by William Caxton at Bruges c.1474 or 1475. The pieces from left to right are king, queen, bishop, knight, rook and pawn. The rook does not seem to have been represented as a castle until the 1500s.

The next illustration shows a very graceful English regency set that was illustrated in Peter Pratt's then anonymous work, *Studies of Chess*, 1804.

Pre-Staunton Chessmen from "1804 Studies of Chess."

19

Staunton Sets

The plate and photo show pieces from a genuine Staunton set; it is the same make as Fischer and Spassky used during their 1972 match at Reykjavik. With some variations the pattern is the only one in use in current

international and other serious competitive chess. The pieces are of UK design and manufacture. Nathaniel Cook conceived their form in 1849. It was designed in simple and unmistakable form to counter-act the prevalent refusals to play with pieces of varying shapes, often difficult to distinguish, which were then available.

Cook registered the design, but three years later came to an agreement for the signature of Howard Staunton to appear in facsimile on the boxes, Staunton being the leading English player of the age. Cook's business was taken over by the then Hatton Garden and now Croydon firm, John Jaques and Son. The firm continues to this day to produce these beautifully proportioned sets. How can one dare make a bad move with such pieces?

Though the handcrafted items are in short supply, there are a number of Staunton pattern sets on the market. The photo illustrates a plastic set, manufactured in Hong Kong, with the king $3\frac{3}{4}$ inches high, which is used widely in chess congresses and even in British Championship contests. They are cheap, well-finished; but for long games I wish the white pieces

in their ivory sort of shade could be softened even more. The sharp contrast between black and white pieces and also the black and white squares is too hard on the eyes—manufacturers please note.

lowing show two such sets in that vanishing material. A lovely contemporary set in silver is depicted overleaf. Made by Gerald Benney (Mr. Winter), it won an award in the silversmiths' competition sponsored by the Arts Council and organised by the Goldsmiths' Company in 1970. Then there is a splendid clear and blue crystal set.

From the earliest times beautiful chess sets have been fashioned from ivory and some of the most beautiful sets have been created. Photos fol-

Special vertical demonstration boards have been designed for the benefit of audiences; these are usually magnetic. In addition there is a great variety of pocket and travelling sets in the shops in which magnetic pieces are the commonest components.

Chess Clocks

The photograph shows a special chess clock. It is two clocks within one frame; each player has a separate clock. Chess clocks are constructed so that only one clock can be in motion at any one time; when the player presses the button above (nearest) his clock, it stops his own clock and starts that of his opponent ticking. The opponent thinks, makes his move and then presses the button nearest him; that stops his clock and, at the same time, starts the other. His clock has recorded the actual time that he spent on the move.

If the game is important the players will usually have agreed to a time limit in which forty moves have to be made in 2 or $2\frac{1}{2}$ hours. The players write down the moves as they are played on a scoresheet. (See p. 12. N.B. The Réti-Alekhine game, recorded on the scoresheet, is one of the finest ever played; it contains what is possibly the longest combinative sequence.) Clocks add both to the tension and excitement of a game. Players often become acutely short of time, so much so that they have to move instantaneously for many moves. What we call a flag, at the top of each clock, is the final arbiter of when the hour is reached. As the hour is approached, the flag is pushed up gradually by the minute hand to a horizontal position; at the moment the hour is reached the flag falls; a player must have made the required number of moves before it falls—failure to do so means the loss of the game.

3 Basis for attack

Among Mates—The Queen

To give checkmate with king and queen against king should be easy. Diagrams 64–68 show the basic mating positions. There are five of them; notice that they all involve the white king.

If you have to mate with king and queen against lone king, you will have to reach one of those basic positions. The king was driven to the edge of the board in each case. The attacking king was needed to stop the prey escaping away from the edge.

Now for an example of how this is done. Have a look at diagram 69. It's White to play. He should be able to force checkmate in about 8 moves. That's 7 moves each, and by the next move White should have given checkmate. Try to work out ways of tackling this ending for yourself before reading any further.

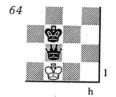
64

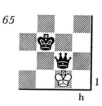
65

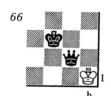
66

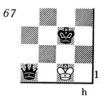
67

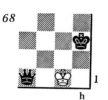
68

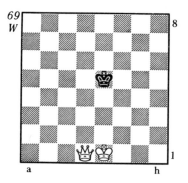
69
W

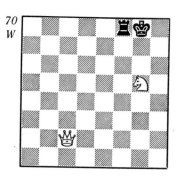
70
W

But remember not to stalemate the black king. Just avoid the positions in diagrams 61 and 62.

Did you manage to mate in 8 moves? What method did you develop? One of the hallmarks of a master is the precision and economy with which he tackles even the simplest tasks.

This is the way I would set about the queen ending. In all the basic positions the king was mated on the edge of the board. Therefore it must first be driven there, and for this both king and queen are needed. I start with **1 Kf2**, and Black would probably reply **1 . . . Kf5**, trying to stay away from the edges; I still advance my king: **2 Kf3**, and Black naturally stays around the centre: **2 . . . Ke5**. Now that I cannot make progress with my king, I look for the most restricting queen move—**3 Qd7**; when Black tries **3 . . . Kf6** my king can sweep forward again—**4 Kf4**. Black has only **4 . . . Kg6**. Again my king cannot advance, so I play another limiting queen move—**5 Qe7**. In reply Black should play **5 . . . Kh6** (the other king move lets White mate in one). Once more the white king can edge closer, **6 Kf5**, there being no stalemate. The black king is left with **6 . . . Kh5** and White has the choice of two mates—**7 Qh7** or **7 Qg5**.

Did you notice that White's first check with the queen was the one that gave mate? Priority was given to bringing up the slow but necessary king.

Complex Mates

More often than not, however, a game will not reach such a simple ending. From mates with very reduced material, let us see how to pluck mates from the most complicated positions.

First you must be able to recognise the essentials of likely mates—a king checked, with flight squares covered or blocked. We have seen basic mates with king and queen versus king, but it won't happen very often that the king is active in complicated middle-games. More likely partners for the queen are the knight, the bishop and the rook.

Take the position in diagram 70: White can play **1 Qh7** mate. Let's merge this into a game position (see diagram 71); it's still **1 Qh7** mate. But in diagram 72, Black has a knight at f6 covering h7, so if White's queen is played to h7 it can be captured. White needs to eliminate the defending knight: he could play **1 Nd5!** (see diag 73). This attacks both Black's key defender (the knight on f6) and his queen. Black cannot afford to take: 1 ... N×d5 2 Qh7 mate. He must save the queen, yet if we move it, **1 ... Qd8**, White will play **2 N×f6+** and after **2 ... Q×f6** comes the planned **3 Qh7** mate.

In diagram 74, it is Black to move. The white king's position has some gaps and possible weaknesses around it. Can Black create mating possibili-

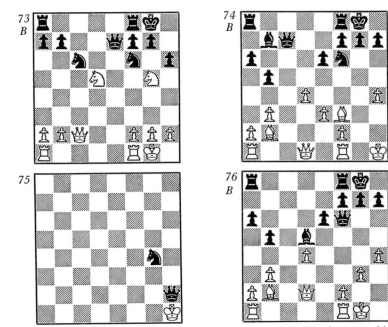

ties? What pieces will have access to the neighbourhood of the target king? What pieces are bearing or can be brought to bear on that area? What basic position is available? Can Black achieve the same end position as in diagram 75? Returning to diagram 74, can the black knight be moved to the same square as in that basic position? Yes, after **1 ... Ng4**, the knight is safe as White's bishop is tied to the diagonal b7–h1 because of the pin. Has White a defence? A king move still allows mate. Nothing can be interposed between the black queen at c7 and the square h2. And there is no counter-threat; White cannot stop the mate.

One is immediately struck by the white-square weaknesses around White's king in diagram 76. Black has a bishop (on d5) overseeing some of those squares (h1, g2, f3). The basic mate position (diag 77) may suggest itself to you. You can super-impose it on your image of the complete position (diag 78). Can it be brought about? The queen joins the bishop's

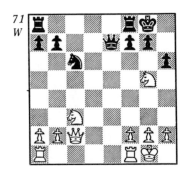

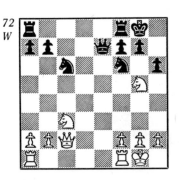

25

77

78

diagonal by **1 . . . Qf3**, and White has no defence to **2 . . . Qg2** mate, and only one defence to the alternative **2 . . . Qh1** mate.

Diagram 79 shows a position that arose in the 1973 Hastings international tournament. White, the Swedish grandmaster, Andersson, played **1 Q×c7??** He had overlooked the possibility of a bishop mate. What did William Hartston, the 1973 British Champion, who was Black, now play? After **1 . . . Qh3+!** Andersson resigned. He saw that if **2 Kh1** there would come **2 . . . Qf1+ 3 Bg1 Q×f3** mate, while **2 K×h3** leads to the mate by **2 . . . Bf1!**

You would look to see how to increase your attacking prospects on the king's side if you had the black pieces in diagram 80. Can you imagine the queen and pawn basic mate? See diagram 81! So in the complex position, Black can push the pawn, **1 . . . f3**, which threatens to reach the basic mate.

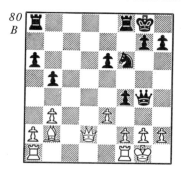

79
W

80
B

81

26

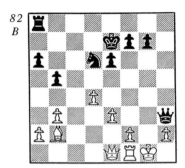

82
B

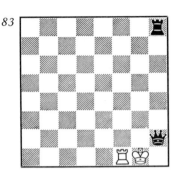

83

84

Rook Mates

From the previous examples, you could quite correctly deduce that a lot of mates are administered to kings stationed on the edge of the board or in the corner. But the queen is by no means the only piece that inflicts those mates. Here are some basic positions with a rook mating.

Diagram 85 shows the king helping; this is useful to know as it is the position to aim for when mating in the ending king and rook versus king.

The mate with two rooks has already been shown in chapter 1, from diagram 19.

Diagram 86 shows an analogous mate with Black's escape blocked by his own pawns; and a fairly similar position using a queen, with its diagonal coverage, is seen in diagram 87.

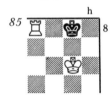

85

h

8

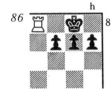

86

h

8

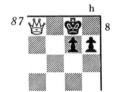

87

h

8

Diagram 88 shows the rook supported by the bishop; the rook and knight mate, shown in diagram 89, is called the 'Arabs' mate' from being possible in pre-European chess; the moves of the rook and knight are the only ones to remain unchanged.

In the next basic position (diag 90) the black king has a flight square open (h7) and can escape from the check. Going one step further, diagrams 91, 92, 93 present White controlling the escape square respectively with his bishop, knight and pawn.

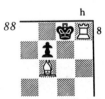

88

h

8

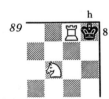

89

h

8

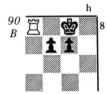

90
B

h

8

White can only stop it by **2 g3**, but Black can still reach the basic mate. He, with **2 . . . Qh3**, slips round White's g-pawn; White can no longer postpone the mate.

We are still looking for mates; see diagram 82. Black can check (1 . . . Qg4+) and check (2 . . . Qf3+) and keep on checking with the queen. That would be a draw; to give mate the queen will need assistance. Which black piece should we choose: the knight or the far-away rook? Which basic mate involves a rook? (Look at diagram 83.) That should suggest the idea of playing **1 . . . Rh8** and, suddenly, White is lost; he cannot stop 2 . . . Q×h2 mate; not even if he moves the f-pawn (see diagram 84).

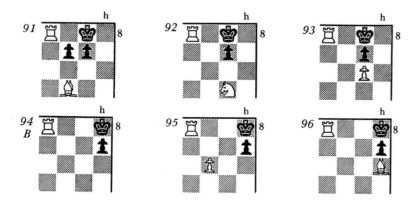

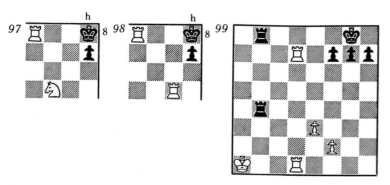

Black escapes from the corner in diagram 94 by . . . Kg7. This escape would not be possible if White had a pawn at f6 (diag 95), bishop at h6 (diag 96), a knight at f5 (diag 97) or a rook at g5 (diag 98).

These by no means cover all the checkmating positions in which a rook is used, but they give a fair range of them. The following two positions give practical examples.

Black, if it was his turn to move, would mate by **1 . . . Ra4** in diagram 99; but, if it was White's turn, mate can be forced by **1 Rd8+ R × d8 2 R × d8**. In the next diagram (100), Black's back row has been strengthened—he has two rooks guarding it; queens have also been added and the white king has

an extra pawn (a2) for shelter. Nevertheless, Black, has in essence, the same mate as in the previous position, viz. **1 . . . R × a2+ !**, removing the White king's cover, **2 K × a2 Qa6**. And have you found the same mate again for White? After the preliminary forced removal of one of the rooks, **1 Q × b8+ ! R × b8**, Black's back row is again inadequately guarded, and White has **2 Rd8+ R × d8 3 R × d8**.

Bishop Mates

Here are some basic bishop mates. In diagram 101 the white king can be played to g1. In diagram 102 this flight square is occupied by his own bishop, while in diagrams 103, 104, 105, 106, 107 and 108 the escape is cut off by a variety of black pieces. The next basic diagram (109) shows a queen

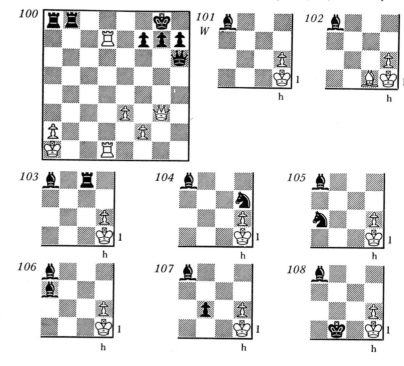

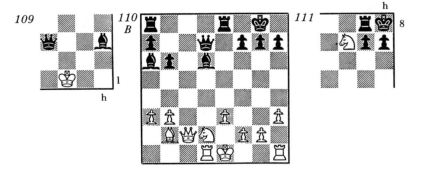

109 | 110 | 111

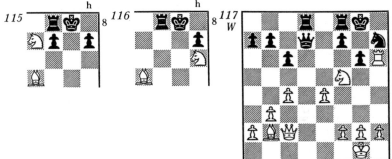

115 | 116 | 117

and bishop inter-acting to give mate. This idea is carried into the next position (diag. 110); if White had no pawn at f2, Black could play . . . Bg3 mate. How can Black force this mate? Answer: **1 . . . R × e3+ 2 f2 × e3 Bg3**.

Knight Mates

Kings are most vulnerable to mate when on a corner square as from there they normally have the least number of neighbouring squares to which to flee. Here are four samples. The smothered mate shown in diagram 111 is the most distinctive, the black king being entirely hemmed in by its own men. In the next three (diags 112, 113 and 114) the escape squares are covered by a rook, a queen and by a knight. The next two positions (diags 115 and 116) show a bishop helping the knight. And this provides the lead-in to the following game position (diag 117); the white rook occupies the square needed by the knight to give checkmate; **1 R × g6+** is the most forceful way for the rook to be got out of the way; after **1 . . . f7 × g6** White mates by **2 Nh6**.

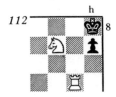
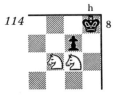
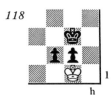

112 | 113 | 114

A Pawn Mate

Pawns can also give mate (diagram 118 is an example) but such happenings are rare.

As an example of play laced stiffly with early checkmates, there is this game published by the Italian, Gioachino Greco, in the early 1600s: **1 e4 e6 2 d4 Nf6 3 Bd3 Nc6 4 Nf3 Be7 5 h4 0–0 6 e5 Nd5 7 B × h7+ K × h7 8 Ng5+**—diagram 119; then Black has five possible replies.

Don't be surprised that, when the king comes forward, it receives rough treatment. If 8 . . . Kh6 then White can uncover check by the bishop (on c1) on to the black king by moving the knight, and would look around for the best way for the knight to inflict damage on to Black's position. Soon he

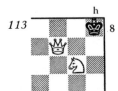

118

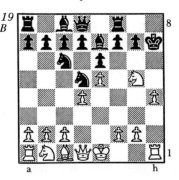

119

would find that he could win the black queen by double check (9 Nf7++).
And 8 . . . Kg6 could be even worse; there's 9 h5+ Kf5 10 g4 mate. If
8 . . . Kh8, White mates by 9 Qh5+ Kg8 10 Qh7—one of our basic set-ups.

One of the two serious defences is 8 . . . Kg8; White would play 9 Qh5
to threaten 10 Qh7 mate, with the variation 9 . . . Bb4+ 10 c3 Re8 11
Q×f7+ Kh8 12 Qh5+ Kg8 13 Qh7+ Kf8 14 Qh8 +Ke7 15 Q×g7 mate.
The other serious defence occurred in the game; Black played 8 . . . B×g5,
allowing White to open the rook's file 9 h4×g5+ and after 9 . . . Kg8,
White, by 10 Qh5 has a mate in the offing (11 Qh8—queen supported by
rook). By 10 . . . f5, Black opened an escape route, which White plugged
with 11 g6. Black played 11 . . . Re8 and White mated 12 Qh8.

One more game: 1 e4 e5 2 Nf3 d6 3 Bc4 Bg4 4 Nc3 White is bringing
his men into action quickly. 4 . . . h6? This is bad because it doesn't help
to develop his pieces. White can now win a pawn. 5 N×e5! White offers
his queen as he has a mate in mind. 5 . . . B×d1? Comparatively best for
Black is to take the knight and allow White to take the bishop. 6 B×f7+
Ke7 7 Nd5 checkmate. This is known as Légal's Mate, after a French
player of two hundred years ago. For a change the king is neither on the
edge nor in the corner of the board.

Tactical Weapons
You should store in your memory some hint of every tactical device remotely
likely. Without such a fund of ideas, based on the collective skill of generations of players, it is possible to stare at the chessboard for a long time, and
still not see an otherwise obvious solution to the problems of the position.

The first branch of tactics is devoted to forms of double attacks; exploiting positions where one move attacks two targets simultaneously.
The simplest form is the fork, which can be carried out by any piece or
pawn.

Forks
Diagram 120 illustrates a knight fork—the white knight is attacking both
the black king and rook; the king moves and then White may take the rook.

In diagram 121 we see the knight forking king and queen. Can you transfer

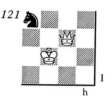

this idea to the position in diagram 122, in which it's Black to move? Black
obtained a winning material advantage with 1 . . . B×f2+. The bishop is
forking the white king and queen. If 2 K×f2, Black again forks king and
queen, by 2 . . . N×e4+; and if 2 Q×f2 then 2 . . . Nd3+; in both cases
White loses his queen.

The following short game was won by Jonathan Penrose, who was British
champion ten times during the twelve year period 1958 to 1969; he was
Black. 1 d4 Nf6 2 c4 e6 3 Nf3 d5 4 g3 dc 5 Nbd2 c5 6 dc White is playing
too passively. 6 . . . B×c5 7 Bg2. Now Penrose initiated a decisive attack
based on knight forks. 7 . . . B×f2+ 8 K×f2 Ng4+ (diag 123). This
check leaves White three possibilities. If 9 Kf1 Black has the knight fork
9 . . . Ne3+. If 9 Kg1 Black forces mate with 9 . . . Qb6+. White played
9 Ke1 but resigned after Penrose's reply—9 . . . Ne3; his queen is lost. If
10 Qa4+ then 10 . . . Bd7 forces either 11 Qa3 or 11 Qb4, and in both
cases Black has 11 . . . Nc2+ and captures the queen next move.

The position in diagram 124 illustrates one of the most common types

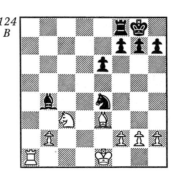

of bishop fork: after Black plays **1 . . . N×c3**, if White recaptures, **2 bc**, Black, by **2 . . . B×c3+**, forks king and rook.

Diagram 125 shows the two-pronged possibilities of a king journey. It is Black to move; he needs to stop White's a-pawn from queening on a8, and he can win it by a direct approach (**1 . . . Kb3**) and take it on his next move. In the meantime, however, the white king would be winning Black's remaining pawn and preparing to promote his own e-pawn. White would then win; but in fact, by a little ingenuity, Black can turn the tables. His king takes six moves to reach a8—sufficient to stop White's a-pawn—whether it travels via b3–b4–b5–b6–b7–a8 or d3–e4–d5–c6–b7–a8; therefore Black can remove both white pawns by the second journey, and win!

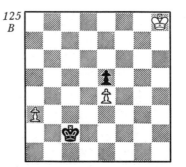

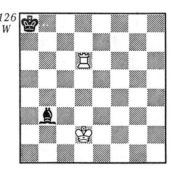

After **1 . . . Kd3!** White can try two plans, but they both fail:

a) **2 a4 K × e4 3 a5 Kd5 4 a6 Kc6 5 a7 Kb7 6 a8=Q+ K × a8** or

b) **2 Kg7 K × e4 3 Kf6 Kd4 4 Kf5 e4 5 Kf4 e3 6 Kf3 Kd3** and Black is winning.

I would like to illustrate a pawn fork by these opening moves: **1 e4 e5 2 Nc3 Nf6 3 Bc4**. Now Black can soundly and usefully play **3 . . . N × e4** as after the recapture, **4 N × e4**, Black has the pawn fork **4 . . . d5** regaining his piece. At the same time, Black is bringing forces—particularly the bishop on c8—into play with increased momentum.

With the aid of forking possibilities by his rook, White can win Black's bishop in the position in diagram 126. After **1 Kc3**, the bishop can move to any one of four squares where it cannot be captured, or, as we say, is not en prise. But White can organise a rook fork in each case: if 1 . . . Ba2 or 1 . . . Ba4 then 2 Ra6+ ; if 1 . . . Bg8, White plays 2 Rd8+. It takes one move longer if Black plays 1 . . . Bf7. White has to check first by 2 Rd8+ and then, after 2 . . . Kb7 or 2 . . . Ka7, 3 Rd7+ wins the bishop.

In diagram 127 the queen fork is one move away. White must eliminate the knight by **1 B × f6** and, after either recapture, continue 2 Qe4, threatening both mate at h7 and, on the other side, the doomed rook on a8.

Pins and Skewers

Other forms of double attack can be against two pieces on the same line. These attacks can be of two kinds, pins and skewers.

Diagram 128 illustrates the pin. The white queen is pinned to the file;

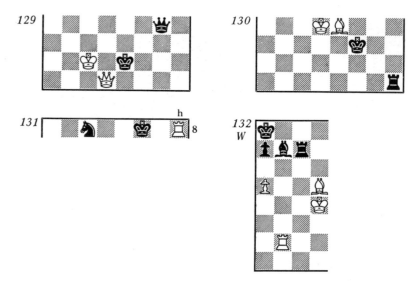

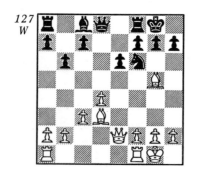

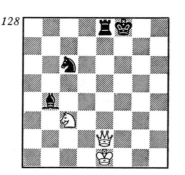

the attempt to move it off the line would expose a more valuable piece, the king, to capture by the black rook. Also, as a further example, the white knight is tied to the diagonal since it is shielding the king from capture.

The other type of double attack along the same line is the skewer, illustrated by diagram 129. In this, a piece is driven off a line, leaving a second piece exposed. Here the white queen is skewering the black king and queen. In diagram 130 the bishop skewers king and rook, while the rook skewers bishop and knight in diagram 131.

The position in diagram 132 is a particularly good example of exploiting a pin. White plays **1 R × b7** as, after the black rook recaptures, **1 . . . R × b7**, it is tied to the diagonal and cannot move, at least for the moment. This gives White the opportunity to play his pawn up, **2 a6**, attacking the rook for a second time, and after **2 . . . Kb8**, take the rook with the pawn.

Without a skewer, the ending in diagram 133 would be difficult to win. With a fine temporary sacrifice of his queen, **1 Qh2+**, forcing **1 . . . Q × h2**, White reaches an ending, which after **2 b8=Q+ K moves** and **3 Q × h2**, should be a matter of technique.

Ambushes

The next class of tactical manoeuvre is the ambushes. This is the form they take: a piece is moved, usually with a threat, uncovering a second piece, which either gives check or has some other separate threat. In diagram 134 White, by moving the bishop, uncovers his rook, which thus gives check to Black's king. To make the move more effective, White plays **1 Bg5++** or 1 Bf2, attacking the black queen and king.

There have been a lot of novices' games that have opened **1 e4 e5 2 Nf3 Nf6 3 N×e5** (diag 135) **3 ... N×e4?** (It is better to play 3 ... d6 first, pushing back the knight.) **4 Qe2 Nf6?** This loses the queen to **5 Nc6+** discovering check from the white queen and attacking the black queen.

White has a very neat example of a discovered attack in the composed

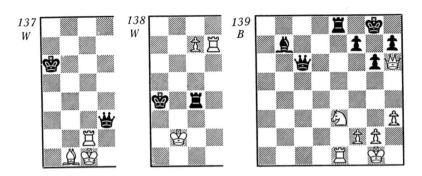

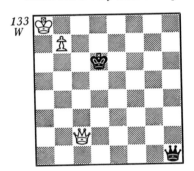

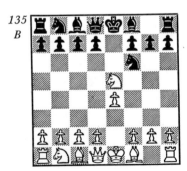

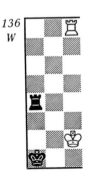

position in diagram 136. By **1 Kb3**, attacking the black rook, White also opens the file for his rook, and threatens 2 Rc1 mate. Black must lose the rook.

In diagram 137, the masking piece moves and gives check, **1 Ra2+**, opening the diagonal of the bishop.

A sample from actual play is **1 e4 c5 2 Nf3 d6 3 d4 cd 4 Nxd4 Nf6 5 Nc3 g6 6 f4 Bg7 7 e5 de 8 fe Ng4**—not best—**9 Bb5+ Kf8** and now White should play **10 Ne6+**, uncovering the white queen on to Black's.

Over-Extended

This complex class of tactical manoeuvres includes deflecting and destroying guards and exploiting overworked pieces. They are related. In diagram 138 a simple example of a guard being forcibly deflected has arisen. The black rook has the all-important job of stopping the white pawn from queening, therefore it must not leave the c-file. But it cannot cope with White's move **1 Rd4**, pinning it along the rank. After **1 ... Rxd4 White queens** the pawn. Queen and king should normally win against rook and king!

When you examine the position in diagram 139, you will find that White's knight has the important role of guarding the g-pawn and stopping Black from giving mate. Black gets rid of the guard by playing **1 ... Rxe3** and White has neither time to re-take nor to defend his rook.

By checking the functions of the black pieces in diagram 140, we will find that Black's rook has two jobs, namely—to protect the pawn at f7, which White is attacking with queen and bishop, and to protect his queen. When it is forced to deal with **1 Bxf7+** by capturing the bishop, it is no longer available to carry out its other duty, so after **1 . . . Rxf7** White wins by **2 Qxd8+**.

We'll take leave of this group with the position in diagram 141, in which a light deflection is nonetheless decisive. If White advances, 1 a6, Black can stop it by 1 . . . Be3 placing his bishop on to the g1–a7 diagonal. The pawn will only be advanced further over the bishop's dead body, Black being willing to give up the bishop for the pawn if necessary, as the draw would then be certain; his king can cope with the g-pawn. White must stop the bishop getting on the g1–a7 diagonal. But how? If 1 Ke4 Black plays 1 . . . Bf8, threatening to join the diagonal at c5. White must drive the bishop on to an inferior diagonal by the pawn sacrifice **1 g5+**. After **1 . . . Kxg5** the black king has got in the way of the bishop, and White can happily push the pawn on to queen—**2 a6, 3 a7** and **4 a8=Q**. And what if 1 . . . Bxg5, the only reasonable alternative? Then 2 Ke4, and once more the black king obstructs its own bishop. The only chance it has of reaching the important a7–g1 diagonal in two moves is by 2 . . . Bh4, but when White puts paid to all tries with 3 Kf3, Black can resign. The pawn cannot be stopped.

Sabotage

The next grouping would seem to be an anarchist's dream—the creation of traffic jams and obstructions! Usually these are evolved from simple interpositions.

Diagram 142 demonstrates an example of successful interposition. White would like to queen the pawn without giving Black the chance to exchange his rook for it. He can bring the knight to c8, shutting out Black's rook by aid of **1 Ne7+**, and after the king moves, White's knight interposes (2 Nc8) and his pawn should queen next move.

With the position in diagram 143, we graduate to downright obstructiveness. White wants to push his sole remaining pawn home to queen, but, if 1 a7, Black easily stops it with the diagonal-opener 1 . . . d4, after which White has no hope of advancing the pawn and keeping the queen. Yet by playing first **1 Bd4**, White ensures that the diagonal is blocked for at least three moves.

It was the Estonian grandmaster, Paul Keres, who constructed the obstacle course in diagram 144. White, with only king and bishop, has to play and mate the black king in four moves. It's done by inducing Black to get his pieces hopelessly entangled. After 1 Bd2, Black stops mate by 1 . . . Rc7. If instead, the bishop had gone to e3, 1 . . . Rd7 would have kept the bishop out of the crucial a1–h8 diagonal, while, if 1 Bf4, then 1 . . . Nf7 holds up the bishop. The solution is **1 Bg5!** threatening 2 Bf6, and after **1 . . . Rf7** (necessary), the knight can no longer go to that square. Now

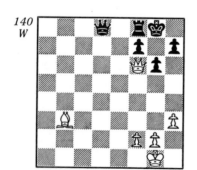

141
W

142
W

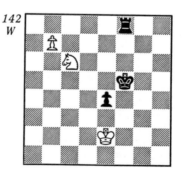

143
W

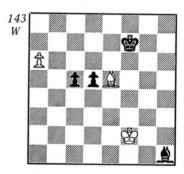

2 Bf4 forces **2 ... Nc6** where it blocks the c-file, and only now **3 Bd2**, as no black piece can reach the c3 square to prevent mate next move.

Diagram 145 embodies an open/shut manoeuvre. Black by **1 ... b3** opens the diagonal for his queen to go to e1, shuts White's queen out from the defence of a2, and incidentally threatens **2 ... Qxa2 mate!** White has no good defence.

A particularly flamboyant example of obstruction or line interference occurs in diagram 146. Examining the roles of the black pieces we find that the bishop, besides attacking the white rook, is stopping the white a-pawn queening at a8, while the black rook is stopping the other white pawn on e7. The routes for the two black pieces intersect at d5. White therefore parks his rook on this junction square—**1 Rd5!!** If the bishop takes, the rook is blocked, and White queens the d-pawn with check (1 ... Bxd5 **5 d8=Q+**); if rook takes (1 ... Rxd5), the a-pawn queens (**2 a8=Q**). The experts call this a Nowotny Interference. It's a rarity, but nevertheless revealing.

Clearances

The opposite of obstructions are the vacating of squares and the clearance of lines.

In diagram 147, Black's bishop on f2 occupies the square which Black would like to be free for his knight to go to and fork White's king, queen and rook. If he looks around for the most effective bishop move, he will quite likely come up with **1 ... Bxg3!** etc.

There are various ways of clearing lines. The example in diagram 148, was specially composed to illustrate the *Bristol clearance*. White vacates the queening square for his pawn and clears most of the diagonal by **1 Bg2**; Black follows similar reasoning with his long bishop move, **1 ... Bh8**. Play would continue with mutual pawn promotions **2 a8=Q a1=Q**. Now with queen following its bishop right down the diagonal, **3 Qf3**, White threatens mate by **4 Qg4**. Black stops it by the Bristolian move **3 ... Qg7**, but now White moves **4 Bf1**, planning 5 Be2, with 6 Qf2 or 6 Qe1, mating, to follow.

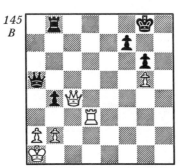

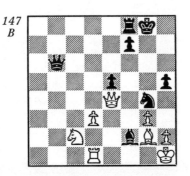

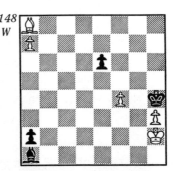

Forcing Moves

From clearing the arteries I move on to forcing sequences like checks, the attack of a weaker unit on to a more powerful one, mate threats and so on, and to sandwich moves—those interpolations which can suddenly alter the nature of a position. Vacating squares can be one aspect of a sandwich move. In diagram 149 the black knight is forking the two white rooks but White escapes with 1 Re8+, and after 1 . . . Kh7 moves his other rook out of danger.

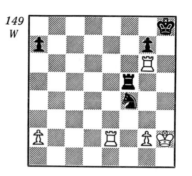

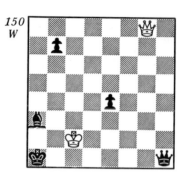

Like all other moves, checks should be played with a purpose. Don't check for the sake of checking! Do you remember the queen and king versus king ending two chapters ago? Plenty of checks available, but none were given—until mate. In our next position (diag. 150) White has plenty of checks, each one drawing the net tighter around the black king. They go **1 Qg7+, 2 Qf7+, 3 Qf6+** and the white queen continues checking down the staircase (**4 Qe6+, 5 Qe5+, 6 Qd5+, 7 Qd4+, 8 Qc4+, 9 Qc3+, 10 Qb3+**) with the black king monotonously alternating between a2 and a1. Eventually White mates by **11 Qxa3**.

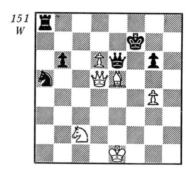

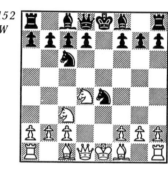

Diagram 151 contains a fine example of a sandwich move (or an in-between move, or an intermediate move) or the German form used among many expert players—the *zwischenzug*. If White takes the rook straight away (1 Qxa8) Black has the adequate reply of 1 . . . Qxe5+ and will be in no danger of losing. But White has the sandwich move **1 Qf3+** forcing Black's king back either to e8 or to g8, when White can take the rook with check (**2 Qxa8+**) and thus remain with an extra bishop.

The 'desperado' combination is part of the sandwich move scene. Consider the sequence **1 e4 e5 2 Nf3 Nc6 3 Nc3 Nf6 4 d4 ed 5 Nxd4**. If a piece is going to be lost next move or so, one looks around for the most advantageous way of selling it. In this game Black's next move, 5 . . . Nxe4?! (diag 152), is based on the pin 6 Nxe4? Qe7, as Black has on White's 7 Nxc6 the sandwich 7 . . . Qxe4+, coming out a pawn up. Instead the game could go **6 Nxc6!** and now the series of desperado moves: **6 . . . Nxc3 7 Nxd8 Nxd1 8 Nxf7 Nxf2 9 Nxh8 Nxh1** and the game continues **10 Be3!** with chances for both players. This fantastic sequence of combinations actually occurred in a 1949 West German championship game.

Promotion

The promotion of a pawn must be regarded as one of the best ways of gaining a material advantage. Take the confrontation here of three pawns against three (diag 153). It is White to move. Can he organise a breakthrough? Seemingly not, but perhaps he can create a gap? After **1 b6!** Black with either his a- or c-pawn; which, is of no importance here, so we'll play **1 . . . ab**. Now, if Black had no pawn on b7, the white a-pawn would sail through; the b7 pawn is diverted by the second sacrifice **2 c6**—threatening 3 cb and queening on the following move. Therefore **2 . . . bc 3 a6** and White queens long before one of Black's pawns can do.

The difference in value between a pawn and a queen is the incentive for all sorts of ingenuity in getting a pawn home. In the position in diagram 154,

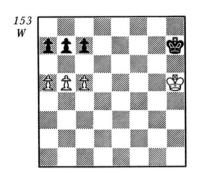

153
W

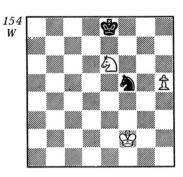

154
W

155
W

Nets

Besides nets weaved to mate the king, ways of netting all the other pieces have to be looked out for. Here in diagram 156 the knight traps the rook in the corner (White threatens N × a8). In the next position (diag 157), White's bishop is trapped after 1 . . . b5 2 Bb3 c4 etc. This has happened to chess novices from time immemorial: hence its popular name, the Noah's Ark Trap! In diagram 158 Black's knight has nowhere safe to go and White can win it by 1 g4.

Pieces lying loose (i.e. unprotected) around the board can be a target. In diagram 159 the black rook comes into that category; and White can win it after a series of checks, with the black king having to dodge mates, by **1 Qd5+ Kb1 2 Qe4+ Ka1** or **2 . . . Ka2 3 Qa8+ Kb1 4 Qb8+**.

Forcing a Draw

Besides combinations to augment one's material, tactics can be invoked with the aim of drawing the game. These can involve stalemate, or perpetual checking, or in whittling down material to below what is required to give mate.

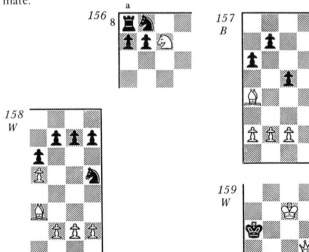

156

157
B

158
W

159
W

the black knight is forcibly deflected to a poor square by White's surprise **1 Ng7+**; after **1 . . . N × g7** comes **2 h6** and Black cannot stop the pawn going on to h8.

Promoting to a lesser piece than the queen is called 'under-promotion'. Sometimes there can be a reason for under-promoting. We might make a rook or bishop when, by promoting to a queen, we would have brought about a draw by stalemate. We can under-promote to a knight because that piece can go to or cover squares that the queen cannot. One under-promotion idea is shown by diagram 155 (something like what happened in one of the games played by the then world champion, Emanuel Lasker, in 1920!). White plays the astonishing **1 Qa7+!** as after **1 . . . K × a7**, the pawn takes the rook and is promoted to a knight, **2 b7 × a8=N+!**, forking king and queen.

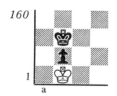

160

161
W

Perpetual check is a common way of forcing a draw. Here are some basic positions. In the first (diag 163), the queen goes back and forth—Qg6 and Qh6; diagram 164 contains a similar theme—1 Qf7+ Kh8 2 Qf8+ Kh7 3 Qf7+ and so on; diagram 165, with Qh5 and Qe8, often occurs. The fourth example of this theme (diag 166) could continue 1 Qf5+ Kg8 2 Qc8+ etc., or break down to a simpler one after 1 Qf5+ g6 and now 2 Q×f7+ Kh8 3 Qf8+ Kh7 4 Qf7+ and so on for ever, or rather for three times, when the draw can be claimed.

Repetition of position is the last factor that I want to look at. Diagram 167 is a position from the 11th game between Spassky, (White), and Fischer, in their 1972 match. Spassky has just played the knight retreat, 1 Nb1, attacking Fischer's queen. Fischer could have played 1 ... Qb2 when it seems Spassky would come into difficulties if he did not repeat the position by 2 Nc3; Fischer would have to go back with his queen 2 ... Qa3, since the threat would be 3 a3 followed by 4 Ra2 trapping the black queen. Instead Fischer went 1 ... Qb4—to avoid the possible draw—and so got into trouble and lost.

We've seen queen and king versus king stalemates and an important one from a pawn ending (diag 160) Take the further position in diagram 161; White to move went **1 Kf8?** and Black sneaked a draw by **1 ... Rf7+** as **2 K×f7** leaves the black king stalemated.

Of course, stalemate cannot be involved in the position in diagram 162. White has lost his queen, but all the other important pieces are still on the board; White has king, two bishops, two knights, one rook and two pawns able to move. Yet White can force Black to stalemate him! After the bishop check, **1 Bh2+**, Black must take, **1 ... R×h2**, and then after **2 Ne2+ K×f5** White, still with six knight moves, three pawn moves and two moves by the bishop, turns them all into statues by **3 g4+ Ke6** and, lo and behold, stalemate!

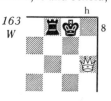

163
W

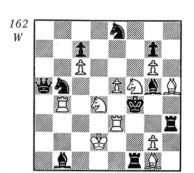

162
W

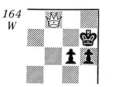

164
W

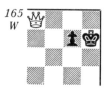

165
W

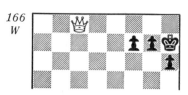

166
W

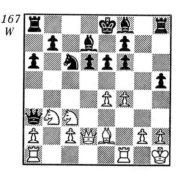

167
W

Attacking the King

Attack may be the best defence, but attacks need a basis: some forces available, some avenues of approach, some weaknesses as targets.

The easiest target is a king. The aim of the attacker will be to build up an overwhelming preponderance of force in the neighbourhood of the opponent's king, and also to destroy or lure away potential defenders.

Alexander Alekhine, the world champion and one of the two finest attacking players of this century, had the white pieces in the position in diagram 168 taken from a 1941 game. All his pieces, except the king rook, are poised for some action on the king-side. He sought out and found the most exact, and really crushing, finish: **1 Qg6!** Black can take with two different pawns: the f- and h-pawns.

White threatens 2 Q×g7 mate. Bar taking the white queen, the only defence is **1 ... Rg8**, when White can mate by 2 Q×h7+, forcing open the h-file; after 2 ... K×h7, 3 Rh3 is mate. It follows that when Black captures the white queen with his h-pawn, **1 ... h7×g6**, the rook move again mates (2 Rh3). In both these cases, the black king's flight square, g8, is covered by the white knight on e7. That leaves only the other pawn capture, **1 ... f7×g6**, but White can still force open the h-line by the knight sacrifice 2 N×g6+. Black's king still cannot flee, as the white bishop on c4 has taken over the role of covering g8; after 2 ... h7×g6, once more, we have 3 Rh3 mate.

The easiest of targets should be the king lacking defensive covering forces.

With both kings wide open in diagram 169, the result depends on which player has the move. Black, to move, would just play 1 ... Ra1 mate. White, if he had the move, would be able to achieve a similar mating set-up, after systematically driving the black king back to the edge. The method is Qe2+ Kf4 2 Rg4+ Kf5 then another left hook from the queen—3 Qe4+—forcing 3 ... Kf6, now a right jab 4 Rg6+, 4 ... Kf7, a left 5 Qe6+. The king is against the ropes, 5 ... Kf8, and the right—6 Rg8— administers mate.

In our diagram 170, Black would like queens to be exchanged. That would leave him a comfortable material advantage, without the present uncertainty stemming from the fact that Black's main forces (queen and rook), are situated on the queen side and may not be adequately supporting the defence of his king. White to move, however, would reject 1 Q×c6?, and possibly investigate the line 1 Q×h7+ Kf8 2 Qh8+ Ke7 3 Qe5+; this would not make him very happy. Then, if he checked the other variation, **1 B×h7+ Kh8**, he would find that, with care, he can force mate by **2 Bg6+** (discovered check from the queen, with the bishop carefully placed to shut off Black's queen) **2 ... Kg8 3 Qh7+ Kf8 4 Q×f7** and that's that.

Smothered Mate

Diagram 171 shows a good example of queen and knight co-operation. They attack together; first comes **1 .. Qc5+**. The White king has to move,

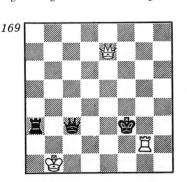

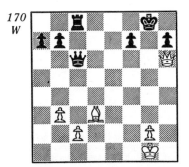

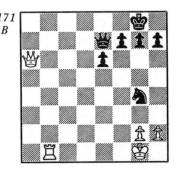

not 2 Kf1 because of 2 ... Qf2 mate, but instead **2 Kh1**. Then, however, **2 ... Nf2+ 3 Kg1 Nh3+** (why this square, will be explained shortly) **4 Kh1** and now Black can force a smothered mate. (The ensuing two-move idea has a name—Philidor's Legacy.) Black starts by sacrificing his queen (**4 ... Qg1+**)—the knight was manoeuvred to h3 in order to make it impossible for White to capture the queen with his king—and after **5 R×g1 Nf2** mates.

King in the Middle
The position in diagram 172 represents another type of attack. The king is caught uncastled, and exposed to attack along open central files. After **1 Re1+ Be7**, White can build up on the pinned bishop by **2 Nd5** while Black can add no more to its protection. His knight is pinned on the b5–e8 diagonal and therefore cannot be interposed at e5. Finally a counter-attack by **2 ... c6**, is too slow: White could continue **3 N×e7 c6×b5 4 Nc6+** (discovered check from the rook) and the black queen is lost.

Into the Breach
Except for the Alekhine position, the four we have shown represent one level at which attacking ideas need to be studied. Now we must progress to a more advanced stage.

One form of successful attack may involve a breaching of the enemy king's fortress, when one has pieces at hand ready to rush in. In diagram 173,

the breaching is effected by a sacrifice of one of White's bishops: **1 B×h7+**. After **1 ... K×h7** White has both queen and rook ready to follow in by **2 Qh5+ Kg8 3 Rh3**, with the threat of Qh7 or Qh8 mate. The only escape for Black's king is via f7 after Black has played **3 ... f6** (or **3 ... f5**) when White can plug the gap by **4 e6**, after which mate will be unavoidable.

An example of a more thorough breaching of the king's position is diagram 174 taken from the 1973 USSR championship. Black played **1 ... N×b6** which means that this knight, momentarily at least, is not available for defence on the king's wing. Gennady Kuzmin, the Soviet's latest grandmaster, didn't bother to recapture, but went for a thorough smash by **2 B×h7+ K×h7 3 Qh5+ Kg8 4 B×g7** sacrificing a second bishop (diag 175). He threatens mate on h8, and to ignore the bishop and play **4 ... f6** allows **5 Qg6** which would clearly be fatal. So Kuzmin's opponent took the bishop, **4 ... K×g7**, and the game was concluded by **5 Qg4+ Kh7 6 Rf3** which threatens to mate after **7 Rh3+**. Black's only way to avoid immediate mate is to play **6 ... Qd8**, giving up the queen (after **7 Rh3+ Bh4 8 R×h4+ Q×h4 9 Q×h4**) when, besides a material disadvantage, his pieces would be poorly mobilised. Black preferred to regard the game as hopeless and resigned it.

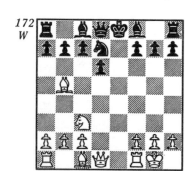

172
W

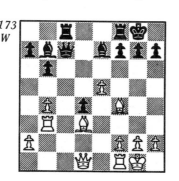

173
W

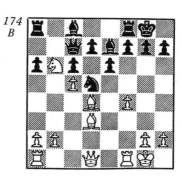

174
B

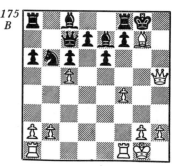

175
B

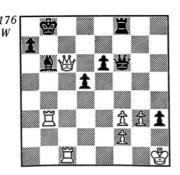

176
W

King Hunt

Diagram 176 gives a relatively modest finish by the great German attacking player of the nineteenth century, Adolf Anderssen. It's a queen and rook finale after the initial sacrifice of rook for bishop (**1 R×b6+ a7×b6 2 Q×b6+ Ka8**). Now White cannot mate immediately by 3 Ra1+, because the black queen would take it. Instead, after **3 Qa6+ Kb8 4 Rb1+**, Black had to resign. He could see that after 4 . . . Kc7 5 Rb7+ Kc8 (or Kd8) 6 Qa8 he would be mated.

A 'king hunt' is a prosaic description of what happens to the black king in the game now to be played through! Perhaps a chess kidnapping, or something sucked out of a quiet chess backyard by a passing tornado, are more appropriate thoughts? It happened in a London club back in 1912. A visiting American engineer, Edward Lasker, had White. **1 d4 f5 2 e4.** He gave up a pawn to speed development of his pieces. **2 . . . f5×e4 3 Nc3 Nf6 4 Bg5 e6** This was rather tame. **5 N×e4 Be7 6 B×f6 B×f6 7 Nf3 b6 8 Bd3 Bb7 9 Ne5** Prepared to play 9 Qh5+ now that the knights and

bishop would be ready to co-operate. Black tried **9 . . . 0–0** but White still replied **10 Qh5**. White wanted to move the knight on e4, anywhere, so as to line up his bishop, as well as the queen, on the h7 pawn. Lasker's opponent played **10 . . . Qe7**, meeting one possibility—now if White played 11 N×f6+ Black could reply by 11 . . . g7×f6 and have his queen covering h7. But now the tornado struck, picked up the the black king and deposited it on White's back row. **11 Q×h7+!** Lasker began by giving up his queen, and after **11 . . . K×h7** played **12 N×f6++.** Double check! Black had to play **12 . . . Kh6** as after 12 . . . Kh8 13 Ng6 would have been checkmate! (diag 177) **13 Neg4+ Kg5 14 h4+ Kf4 15 g3+ Kf3** Every white move was check and every reply of Black's was forced. **16 Be2+ Kg2 17 Rh2+ Kg1** Made it! But there's no reward (diag 178). **18 Kd2** That's it—checkmate. 18 0–0–0 is also mate. White missed two opportunities of checkmating in one move less, but, somehow here it doesn't seem to be a flaw. A fantastic game.

Diagram 179 shows a position taken from the 'Evergreen Game' between Anderssen and Dufresne. Anderssen, on whose prowess as an attacking wizard of the last century I have already commented, had the white pieces. The black king has remained uncastled, in the centre. Anderssen's opponent was relying on his threats to the white king—in particular he is ready to play . . . Q×g2 mate.

Anderssen started his final attack with **1 R×e7+** to which his opponent replied with **1 . . . N×e7**, apparently bringing to an end White's aggressive

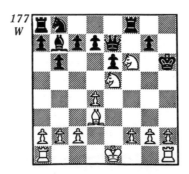

177
W

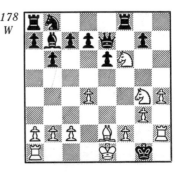

178
W

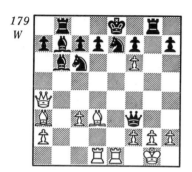

intentions. But Anderssen had in store the stunning queen sacrifice, **2 Q×d7+!!** and Black must take back, since if 2 . . .Kf8 3 Q×e7 is mate. So, **2 . . . K×d7** when **3 Bf5++** followed, and as it is double check, the king must move; if 3 . . . Kc6, White has 4 Bd7 mate; Anderssen's opponent played **3 . . . Ke8**, but now White's two bishops co-operate in a mate by **4 Bd7+ Kf8** (The same happens if it is played to the other square). **5 B×e7** checkmate. That brilliancy was played in Berlin in 1852! This is one advantage that chess possesses, over all other games. Chess games can be written down, and indeed the moves of practically all important games of the last hundred years are available. There are literally thousands of books on chess; and this means we can still learn something from past generations. Our technique, today, may be superior, to that of players of the past, but

our games have been immeasurably enriched by the ideas that we have culled from the great players who have gone before us. Bobby Fischer spent time studying and writing about the 19th century greats.

Genius of Attack

The genius of attack in contemporary chess is the Latvian ex-world champion, Mikhail Tal. I would like to show you how he dealt with a complicated position when he was only twelve years old. Look at diagram 180, where Tal had the white pieces. He boldly played **1 Rf6!**, where it could be taken by two of Black's pieces! His opponent feared the worst and didn't take it. The game continued **1 . . . Qf8 2 Rf4 Bd2 3 Ng4 Be8 4 Nf6+** (Tal is determined that Black should not play 4 . . . f5 to improve his internal com-

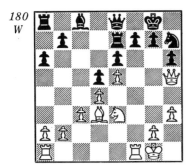

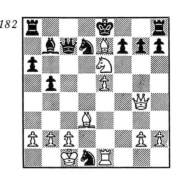

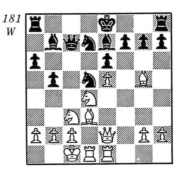

munications). **4 ... N×f6 5 e7×f6 Rc7 6 f6×g7 K×g7 7 Qe5+** ; thus Tal won the rook and the game.

What if Tal's opponent had accepted the rook sacrifice? After 1 ... g7×f6 2 e5×f6 N×f6 3 Q×h6 Ne4 4 B×e4 d5×e4 5 Ng4 Tal would be threatening 6 Nf6+, forking king and queen, as well as mate. Black could not defend himself against both. The game would not yet be over, but White would have the better prospects.

This is the sort of ability that we have to measure our 12- and 13-year-olds against, in assessing their potential for international honours and opportunities. By the age of 23 Tal had won the world championship!

Spassky Attacks

Boris Spassky played the following incisive game against Naum Rashkovsky, when winning the 1973 USSR title. Boris was White.

The opening moves were **1 e2–e4 c7–c5 2 Ng1–f3 d7–d6 3 d2–d4 c5×d4 4 Nf3×d4 Ng8–f6 5 Nb1–c3 a7–a6** (Fischer's favourite defence) **6 Bc1–g5 e7–e6 7 f2–f4 Qd8–c7 8 Bf1–d3 Nb8–d7 9 Qd1–e2 b7–b5 10 0–0–0 Bc8–b7 11 Rh1–e1 Bf8–e7**. Boris has taken only 4 minutes of his allocated 2½ hours for 40 moves, while on his opponent's clock 6 minutes have elapsed. This position is shown in diagram 63. After one minute's thought, Spassky pushed **12 e4–e5** and three minutes later Rashkovsky answered by **12 ... d6×e5**; after two more minutes Spassky re-took— **13 f4×e5**: he is trying to force open all the approach lines to Black's king

at e8. Naum thought for 41 minutes and played the quite aggressive knight move **13 ... Nf6–d5** (diag 181).

For his 14th move Spassky pondered for 46 minutes between the move he played and 14 N×e6 and settled for **14 Bg5×e7**; he would have gone deeply into his following move as well. When, after 5 minutes, Naum took the knight, **14 ... Nd5×c3**, Boris took a further 7 minutes before embarking on the all-out attack with **15 Qe2–g4**. There are many sacrificial lines to be calculated. The long thought by both players has determined the character of the struggle ahead.

The question was 'Who's judgement was right?' I remember a penetrating remark of Fischer's, made a decade ago, to the effect that Spassky was able to sacrifice with complete abandon. This is an example. Boris feels that the black king's insecurity will compensate him for any material losses.

25 minutes later Naum Rashkovsky took the rook—**15 ... Nc3×d1**. Now Boris let the time slip by while he worked out the precise method of attack. It was another 30 minutes on his clock before he played **16 Nd4×e6** (diag 182); 16 Bd6 is possibly more accurate, e.g. 16 ... Qa5 17 Qg5 Qd8 18 Q×g7. Naum took 45 minutes to reply with **16 ...Qc7–c6**; it would have been better to take the knight; he now only had 25 minutes left for 24 moves. Boris spent 27 minutes over **17 Ne6×g7+** ; but now he saw his way through to the end.

Boris's move must have come as a surprise to Naum; although his reply is forced it was 12 minutes before he played **17 ... Ke8×e7**; perhaps the thought of impending defeat was having its impact. Boris took five minutes before playing **18 Qg4–g5+**, met, after a minute's thought, by **18 . . . f7–f6**. Spassky's **19 e5×f6+** took him less than a minute; Naum's clock went on for another 4 minutes before he played **19 . . . Ke7–d8**; again less than a minute before Spassky checked, **20 f6–f7+**; a further 4 minutes. . . .

Rashkovsky moved **20 . . . Kd8–c7**; another minute, and Spassky checked **21 Qg5–f4+**. Rashkovsky stared hard at the position; his queen is lost after **21 . . . Qd6 22 Ne6+ Kc6 23 Be4**; the position is hopeless, and he has 20 moves to find in a minute or two. He knocked over his king—a quite normal procedure—as a token of his resignation.

4 Positional play

Aims of Play

It is appropriate at this stage to issue a general directive of aims for playing a game. I would summarise my approach in the following list:

1 To mate the opposing king;
2 To build up a decisive concentration of pieces on the approaches to the king;
3 To gain an advantage in material that, in time, can be converted into a mating force;
4 To make my pieces work effectively as units and harmoniously as a team;
5 To render the opponent's pieces ineffective;
6 To frustrate the opponent's plans;
7 To draw, if to win is out of the question;
8 Not to lose;
9 If losing, to create chances for the opponent to go wrong;
10 To fight like hell to achieve these objectives;
11 To remain courteous to my opponent.

Pawns—The Soul

Pawns are the soul of chess. So said André Philidor, the dominant French player of two centuries ago. And what he learnt from the writings (1560–1580?) of the Spanish priest, Ruy Lopez, and added to them, has strongly influenced modern play. His games were distinguished through effective cramping by his pawns. The following examples will give some indications of how pawn structures influence piece play.

Pawn Centres

Pawns at e4 and d4 form one typical centre (diag 183); they create a minefield

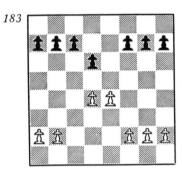

183

(c5/d5/e5/f5) which Black's knights and bishops seeking central posts have to avoid.

The game Leonhardt against Amos Burn in 1911, shows the effect of a mighty pawn centre. It began **1 e4 e5 2 Nf3 Nc6 3 Bc4 Bc5 4 c3 d6 5 d4 ed 6 cd Bb6 7 Nc3 Nf6 8 0–0 0–0**. Now Black threatens the common combination 9 . . . N×e4 10 N×e4 d5 which regains his piece and gets rid of the pawn centre in the process. White avoids this with **9 Bb3** and play continued **9 . . . Bg4 10 Be3 h6**. This is passive; Black would do better to keep White's centre under fire with 10 . . . Re8 11 Qd3 Bh5 and bringing his bishop to g6. The game proceeded **11 Qd3 Re8 12 Nd2 Qe7 13 Rae1 Rad8 14 a3**. With Black's pieces so boxed in, White can leisurely cover and deprive Black of every useful looking square. **14 . . . Qf8 15 f4** White threatens to hem in the black bishop at g4 by f5 followed by h3. Black played

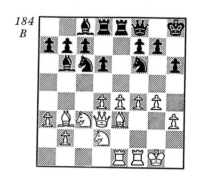

184
B

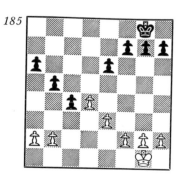

185

15 ... Bc8 and White's game assumed crushing dimensions after 16 h3 Kh8 17 g4. (diag 184) Black tried to break out of the stranglehold by 17 ... Ne7 18 Kh1 d5 but after 19 e5 had a pitiful number of squares available. The game continued 19 ... Nh7 20 f5 f6 21 e6 c6 22 Bf4 Ng8. To have a square for the queen 23 Na4 White threatens 24 N×b6 and then to win bishop for rook by 25 Bc7; there's a battle for some moves over this. 23 ... Ba5 24 Bc2 Qe7 25 Qg3 b5 26 Nc5 Black never escaped from White's grip and was forced to resign 16 moves later.

The battle of differing pawn formations is exemplified by this basic position (diag. 185). White, with the d+e pawns, has a potentially cramping pawn centre; this could also advance and drive a wedge into the black position. Middle game prospects often favour White; but the position of the pieces is a vital factor; if Black survives the middle-game he may be able to create a passed pawn on the Q-side by advancing the pawns to b4 and c3. Passed pawns increase in value as does their distance from the opposing king.

In the position from a grandmaster game between Gligoric (Yugoslavia) and Szabo (Hungary) (diag 186), White's three pawns to one on the queen's wing look very imposing. Play went 11 ... a5 12 Rb1 ab 13 ab Nc6. Now White could be tempted by 14 b5 but then comes 14 ... Ne5 threatening mate (... Nf3) and after 15 f4 Nf3+ 16 Kf2, Black can afford to give up the knight by 16 ... B×c5+ 17 K×f3 as he obtains a great attack with 17 ... d4 opening the diagonal b7–h1. The game continued 14 Bg2 Rb8

15 Ba3 Bd7 16 0–0 Na7. The squares in front of the White pawns will become havens and posts for the black pieces. 17 Re1 Ne8 18 Bc1 Bf6 19 Bf4 e5—first step forward of Black's pawn centre—20 Bd2 d4 21 Nd5 Bc6 22 N×f6+ Q×f6 23 B×c6 Q×c6 24 f4 f6 25 Qb3+ Kh8 26 Rf1 Nc7 White's pawns are firmly held, while Black's pawns are restricting White's knight and bishop. 27 Qc4 Nab5 28 Rbe1 h6 29 g4 Rbe8 30 f5 Exchanging pawns by 30 fe fe would have given White more counterplay. 30 ... Qd4 31 Qc1 Kh7 32 Ng3 e4 These black pawns now dominate the board. 33 Bf4 e3 34 Qd1 Qc4 35 h4 Nd5 36 g5 d3 37 Qg4 Rg8 This rules out any tactical resources along the g-file. 38 Nh5 Re4 39 g6+ Kh8 Now White played 40 Qg3 but conceded the game; he has no good answer to 40 ... d2. The centre pawns have triumphed.

Pawn centres are not always advantageous features. They can become a target, and tie down valuable pieces to defending them. The Russian chess president, Yuri Averbakh, set about destroying the effectiveness of White's pawn centre (diag 187) by the pawn attack 14 ... f5, trying to knock out the middle pawn. If White pushes on (15 e5), then the square d5 becomes available for Black's pieces—bishop, queen and perhaps knight—and Black can also build up pressure on the backward white pawn at d4. The game continued 15 R×c8+ Q×c8 16 Qd2 fe 17 B×e4 Nc4 18 Bd5+ Be6 19 B×c4 Q×c4 when White's pawn centre is broken and weak.

186
B

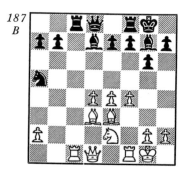

187
B

Pawn Endings

Even reasonably good players miscalculate pawn endings, so one is likely to gain points with even rudimentary knowledge. Diagram 188 gives an ideal position for White. His king stand here ready to shepherd the pawn over the last three fences (f6, f7, f8); Black cannot stop the pawn from queening.

The next diagram (189) is important and critical; what happens depends on whose turn it is to move. If it is White to move he can either play **1 Kf6** leaving the black king stalemated, or write off the pawn. But when it's Black's turn to move he must vacate the queening square, **1 ... Kg7**, allowing White's king to occupy the shepherding position, **2 Ke7**, and then queen.

The next position (diag 190) is an ideal one to be aimed for by the side with the pawn. If the king can reach the sixth rank in front of its pawn (unless the pawn is on an edge file, i.e. an a- or h-pawn), it's a win irrespective of who has the move. When Black moves, for example **1 ... Kg8**, the white king takes the shepherding position **2 Ke7**. With White to move, it's a little more complicated, **1 Ke6 Ke8 2 f6 Kf8 3 f7**, but Black must relinquish his grip on the shepherding square, **3 ... Kg7 4 Ke7**, and White queens.

The move doesn't matter in the next position (diag 191) but accuracy is called for. By **1 ... Ke8** Black would lose after **2 Ke6 Kf8 3 f7 Kg7 4 Ke7** and queens. Instead, Black must step straight back by **1 ... Kf8** so that, after **2 Ke6**, he can go **2 ... Ke8** directly confronting the white king; then

White's attempts to push the pawn home by **3 f7+ Kf8** leads to the loss of the pawn if stalemate by **4 Kf6** is to be avoided. Remember, king straight back ... Kf8, and aim for stalemate.

Again, in diagram 192, the move counts. With it being his turn to move, White is not assured of more than a draw; for example **1 Ke5 Ke7**—confronting directly—**2 f5 Kf7 3 f6** and, as we remember, king straight back by **3 ... Kf8** leads to a draw. With the move Black has to give ground, e.g. **1 ... Ke7 2 Kg6** when White reaches the always winning position with king on the sixth and in front of the pawn.

These five pawn endings should be memorised. Again: from diagram 193, king in shepherding position—a win; from diagram 194, watch for stalemate; king on the sixth in front of the pawn—always a win, that's the lesson of diagram 195; and in diagram 196 king straight back, king up, king confronts (**1 ... Kf8 2 Ke6 Ke8**) ... and draws; another confrontation in diagram 197—if Black must give way he loses.

The exception to these pawn endings are also important. If the defending king can get in front of an a-pawn or h-pawn, the game should always be drawn, due to the increased chances of stalemate.

An important type of pawn ending is shown in diagram 198. White has two pawns to one on the queen's wing and Black three to two on the king's wing. The side that can create a passed pawn and at the same time eliminate all the opposition's pawns on that one wing generally wins. White can play **1 b5+** and bring about such a situation. At the opportune moment, White

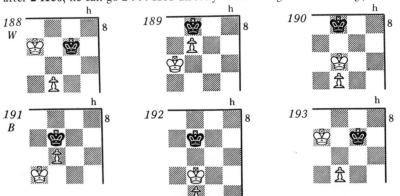

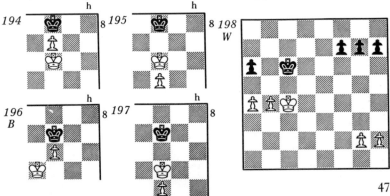

will desert his queen side pawn and proceed to mop up Black's pawns on the king's side.

Pawn Weaknesses

There are a great variety of pawn weaknesses and pawn formations that strongly influence the piece play. From diagram 199, White can give up his fianchettoed bishop at g2—something that is not lightly done—in order to exchange off the knight by **1 B×c6 bc** and weaken Black's pawns. The a7 pawn is isolated from the other pawns; there's no pawn on an adjacent file. The pair at c6 and c5 are doubled and isolated. When this position occurred in a 1954 Russian game, play went **2 Qa4 Qd7 3 Nf3 f6 4 Be3 e5 5 Ne4**

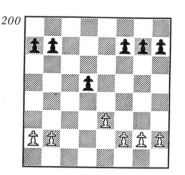

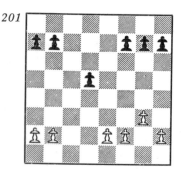

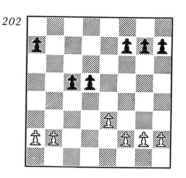

Ne6 6 Rc1 Rb8 7 Qc2 Be7?! 8 N×c5 N×c5 9 B×c5 B×c5 10 Q×c5 R×b2 when Black was suddenly faced with severe problems after the combination **11 N×e5** trying to fork Black's king and rook. White eventually won.

Here are three more basic pawn formations around which are woven many chess battles. In diagram 200, the important feature is Black's isolated central pawn at d5; d5 is also the case in diagram 201; the isolated pawn can be a target, the square in front (d4) a post for an opponent's piece; in favour of it can be greater control its master exercises on the other surrounding squares. The c5+d5 pawns in diagram 202 are described as hanging pawns—there are circumstances where they are strong, and others where they are weak.

Bad Bishop

Black's bishop is badly restricted because his own pawns are fixed on dark squares in diagram 203. There's nothing in White's position that the bishop can bear on, whereas White's knight, on the other hand, can operate from either black or white squares. If White can bring his king to c5 then the black pawns begin to fall. White can try to win this ending because Black's bishop is 'bad'. In an attempt to bring his king to the desired position (c5), White starts with **1 Kb4** and is held up after **1...Kb6**; but **2 Na4+** throws Black more on the defensive, **2...Kc6**, and the white king marginally penetrates Black's territory by **3 Ka5**. From now on White plans to drive the black king back, square by square, and edge his own king to c5. A knight check is required and happens after the manoeuvre **4 Nc3, 5 Na2 and 6 Nb4+**. Black can only mark time. The knight check will lead to White following up with king to b5 and to b6 while the black king retreats to d6. Then the white knight is brought via a2 and c3 to b5 to check once more. This will force the black king out of the d6 square and thus enables the white king to come to c5. Then, after another knight move (c7 or c3) the black d-pawn will fall; White can repeat the approach to Black's remaining pawn.

A simpler, but more improbable, example of a bad bishop is seen in this made up position in diagram 204. The black pieces remain entangled.

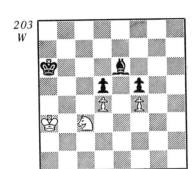

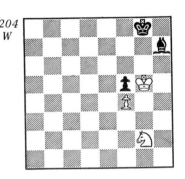

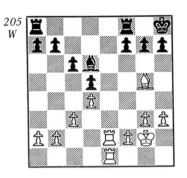

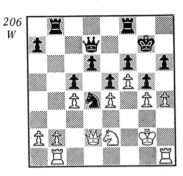

through White's ability to exploit a mating possibility after **1 Kh6 Kh8** with **2 Nh4**; the hoped-for emergence of the bishop into freedom 2 . . . Bg8 would permit the knight mate at g6. Therefore Black must allow White to improve the positioning of his knight **2 . . . Kg8 3 Nf3 Kh8 4 Ne5 Kg8 5 Nc6 Kh8** to **6 Ne7**; then Black, safe as the position stands, has to move and give ground and that means to give up his bishop. For this type of position chessplayers have a special expression—zugzwang—literally meaning move-bound.

Extending the Bishop

After these opening moves: **1 d4 Nf6 2 c4 g6 3 Nc3 d5 4 Bf4 Bg7 5 e3 0-0 6 Nf3** Black, among other things, will not be completely satisfied with the scope of his bishop at g7, and may choose to play **6 . . . c5**, as after **7 dc** the bishop's diagonal is extended and he can bring the queen into co-operative action by **7 . . . Qa5**. Now **8 cd** would be near suicidal because of the line opener **8 . . . N×d5**—if **9 Q×d5 B×c3+ 10 bc** (not best) 10 . . . Q×c3+ when White's rook at a1 goes.

Extending the Rooks

I would like to switch from the use of the bishop to the extension of the rook's development. We seem to have left them sitting at the end of open files waiting for a chance to infiltrate the opponent's territory. In diagram 205, where do you want the white rooks to be? At e7, to get at Black's pawns.

The entry is brought about by **1 Be7** forcing the swap **1 . . . B×e7 2 R×e7**, (b7 pawn is attacked). After **2 . . . Rab8** White can double along the seventh with **3 Rd7** and except at a cost of several pawns, Black cannot stop White following up by the other rook to the seventh, (4 R1e7), when black pawns will fall anyway.

More preparation is involved for the white rooks to break into Black's position in diagram 206. Réti, a great Czech player, who was White, improves everything, ready for the moment of opening up, starting with **1 Nc3**, and this classic game continued **1 . . . Rh8 2 Rh3 Rbg8 3 Rbh1 Qd8 4 Nd5**. Now White wants to play Kf1 for safety reasons, then follow up with hg hg; Qh2 R×h3; Q×h3 Rh8; Q×h8+ Q×h8; R×h8 K×h8 and win the f6 pawn. The game continued **4 . . . gh 5 R×h4 Kf7 6 Kf2 Qf8 7 R×h6 R×h6 8 R×h6 Qg7** when the switch to the alternative way in by **9 Qa5** left Black no suitable reply.

The position in diagram 207 is taken from a world championship game in 1948. Vasily Smyslov—to be world champion in 1957—was White and another equally famous player, Paul Keres, had Black. White would ask himself where his rooks are going to find their needed open file. The half-open c-file offers no immediate targets. Where can pawns be exchanged? At e4, b5 and maybe, but surely unlikely, at a6. Where will it be least helpful to the opponent? Black already has a rook waiting at e8 for the opening of the e-file. Where can the timing be in White's hands? Smyslov played **1 Rab1**! He's planning b2–b4–b5. Play continued **1 . . . Ng6 2 b4 Bd6**

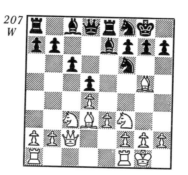

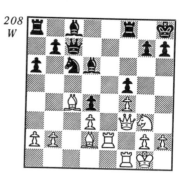

(if 2 ... a6 White can re-inforce his wedge with 3 a4, or if Black blocks with 2 ... b5 perhaps Black's c6-pawn will become a target for White's pieces). The pawn went on **3 b5 Bd7 4 bc**; White had a prolonged initiative and won.

Improving the Knight

After 17 moves, Nimzowitsch-Rubinstein, Dresden 1926, reached the position in diagram 208. Nimzowitsch, not happy with the scope of his knight at g3, looked round for a better square for it. g5 looked good, but how does one bring it there. Nimzowitsch played **18 Nh1!!** He could only be contemplating the journey h1–f2–h3–g5. The game went **18 ... Bd7 19 Nf2 Rae8 20 Rfe1 R×e2 21 R×e2 Nd8** If 21 ... Re8 22 Qd5! Ne7 23 Qf7! wins. **22 Nh3 Bc6** Now 22 ... Re8 is met by 23 Qh5 R×e2 24 Ng5! h6 25 Qg6! forcing mate at h7 or h5. **23 Qh5 g6 24 Qh4 Kg7 25 Qf2! Bc5 26 b4 Bb6 27 Qh4! Re8 28 Re5! Nf7 29 B×f7 Q×f7 30 Ng5** At last **30 ... Qg8 31 R×e8 B×e8 32 Qe1!** This is a splendid example of play for control of the e-file. **32 ... Bc6 33 Qe7+ Kh8 34 b5!!** If now 34 ... ab 35 Ne6 h5 36 Qf6+ Kh7 37 Ng5+ Kh6 38 Bb4! introduces the bishop with decisive effect. **34 ... Qg7 35 Q×g7+ K×g7 36 bc** and won in some moves.

Improving the King

All White's pieces in the position from the Kostich–Capablanca match in

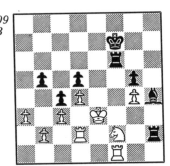

209
B

Bishops of Opposite Colours

The presence of bishops of opposite colours on the board has a distinctive influence. In diagram 210 the ending is drawn as White's bishop is useless for disputing f7 with Black's bishop. In endings bishops of opposite colour are a well-known drawing factor. However, in complex middle game positions, the fact that the bishops are operating on different colour diagonals tends to limit the exchanging off of supporting major pieces (queens and rooks); in such circumstances the bishop on opposite colours can add force to an attack.

Exchanges

Do not shirk the solution of exchanging off an opponent's well placed piece, even queens. It is a common misconception that the game is less interesting with queens off; it is often harder.

Shifting the Emphasis

Wing attacks are best countered by solid distractions in the centre. In his game with Vajda in the match Moscow–Budapest 1949, faced with White's king side pawn storm, (diag 211), the Russian grandmaster, Kotov, successfully shifted the battle arena to the centre by **1 . . . b4! 2 Ne2 e5! 3 f5** if 3 g5 Ng4 4 B×g4 B×g4 5 f5 d5! **3 . . . d5!** Therefore before one embarks on an all-out flank attack one takes steps to have a solid or firm centre.

1919 (diag 209) are tied up by the pins f6–f1 and h2–d2. Capablanca examines the position to find how he can improve his pieces and add to the pressure on Kostich's position. His king is not doing much. If it could be brought all the way to the square b3 then Black could exchange all the pieces off at f2 and help himself to White's queen's side pawn. Capablanca played **51 . . . Ke7!** and he plans then to protect his rook at h2 by . . . Bg3 and after that to proceed with the king's journey. Therefore Kostich tried **52 b4** but after **52 . . . c4×b3 53 Nd3 R×d2** he resigned as after 54 R×f6 Black has the desperado 54 . . . R×d3+! emerging with a bishop up.

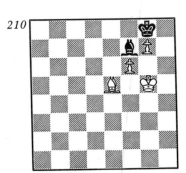

210

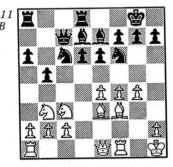

211
B

5 Human factors

Perfect Games are Drawn

The main battle of the chessboard is within yourself! You lose because you make mistakes or you fail to adjust yourself to changes in the nature of the position or the conditions. And you'll do your utmost to prove that some factor external to your brain was responsible for the failure. It is a basic assumption that a chess game cannot be lost without the making of a traceable error.

A perfectly played game should end in a draw. Somewhere between the playing of moves by White and Black, usually after Black's, a state of balance exists. From this players develop a sense of balance that provides the 'feel' of the position. The tilting of this balance will help one to decide whether to play to win or to draw or to complicate or on what other decision arises.

A well-fought draw may be artistically satisfying. That for instance would apply to the game Geller–Golombek played in the big Budapest tournament in 1952; it went **1 d4 Nf6 2 c4 e6 3 Nc3 Bb4 4 e3 c5 5 a3 cd 6 ab dc 7 Nf3!? cb 8 B×b2 d5 9 c5 b6?!9 . . . 0–0** is safer. **10 Bb5+**, possibly better is 10 Bd3. **10 . . . Bb7 11 B×d7+ Nf×d7! 12 Qc2! Nc6! 13 B×g7 N×b4! 14 Qb1 Rg8 15 c6! N×c6 16 Q×h7 Nf6!!** diag 212 **17 B×f6 Q×f6 18 Q×g8+ Kd7 19 Ne5+! N×e5!** If 19 . . . Q×e5 20 Q×f7+ wins. **20 Q×a8 Nf3+ 21 gf.** On 21 Ke2 Qb2+ 22 K×f3 Qf6+ perpetually checks. **21 . . . Q×a1+ 22 Ke2 Qb2+** Draw agreed. It's also perpetual check after 23 Kf1 Qb1+ 24 Kg2 Qg6+ 25 Kh3 Qh5+.

Need for Creative Ideas

But success in chess is measured by the scoring of wins. And that requires imperfections and the intrusion of human factors.

Where two players are well-matched in knowledge, technique and temperament, success still may go to the one who is able to conjure forth time-consuming problems at critical junctures and in general to create

sound new positional and attacking ideas. And that is what top class chess is about.

Over the years the pieces and the board remain the same; there are certain areas of knowledge, particularly in the endings, which are accepted as fact; certain moves in the openings lead to palpably lost positions or mate— these are known and avoided. But there are very large 'grey' areas where certainties do not exist and in which the great players, whose characteristics are so different, can impose, change and refute ideas and approaches. In other words there is a constant flux within chess that keeps it very much alive. For example the openings of today may be has-beens tomorrow.

212
B

PROCEDURE FOR THINKING
Probing the Position
What is he trying to do? This is the number one question in chessplaying. You have to ask yourself this, every time your opponent moves. There are varying shades of this question which could, for instance, depend on whether you are attacking or defending. The great players, even when they move in a flash, will still have asked themselves this question.

Every move adds to the pressure on some square(s) and subtracts from the pressure against others. Look every time, even if only for a fraction of a second, at each fresh square attacked by the piece the opponent's hand has just quitted. By feeding your brain with this information and by asking a series of questions, you develop a sense of the balances and imbalances within a position.

Let's look at an interesting game and examine some of the thinking processes behind the moves. After **1 e2–e4 e7–e5 2 Ng1–f3 Nb8–c6 3 Bf1–c4,** this bishop move adds pressure to the squares b3/d5/e6/f7/f1; it also weakens the hold on g2/h3 and c4. N.B. A piece occupying a square does not control it.

In return for information the brain's thinking centres may provide an almost instant reply. And more than 50 per cent of the time this will be the move you will finally end up by playing. But—a very big but—it rarely pays to accept the first reaction and make a quick move on the board. You are not playing good chess if one move in every three is a bad one. There are further questions and probing to which the first reaction should be exposed. In this, human qualities like courage, recklessness, resolution, timidity, will play an important role.

I want to concentrate on the steps required to develop depth in both reflective thinking and actual calculation. You should learn, when looking at each square newly controlled—either before your own or after his move—to visualise the piece as going to that square and to scan (in your mind) the further squares that could be controlled. One's brain quickly learns to reject the ridiculous and improbable in a matter of hundredths of a second. The second and natural extension deeper is to trace paths for each of one's chessmen and to visualise and create ideal lines of action and posts for them.

You would be advised to do this for your opponent's pieces as well.

To continue our game **3 . . . Bf8–c5 4 c2–c3 Ng8–f6 5 d2–d4 e5 × d4 6 c3 × d4 Bc5–b4+ 7 Nb1–c3 Nf6 × e4.** . . . In trying to reach a decision on what to play here, White may take into account that the ideal positioning for his rook at h1 would be at e1 with pressure directed along the e-file towards the black king. . . . **8 0–0** White threatens Nc3 × e4.

You feed as much relevant data as possible into your thinking centres and hope they will connect up various features of the position and help you to make plans.

The game—**8 . . . Ne4 × c3**—bishop takes, is more usual—**9 b2 × c3 Bb4 × c3?** It should be too risky for Black to go picking up pawns and leaving his main forces at home. A strong player would choose **9 . . . d7–d5** instead It being his move the white player should ask the following questions.

The Questions

First question: What is Black trying to do? Answer: He would like to take my rook in the corner.

Second question: How does Black's capture affect my plan? Answer: I can't play Re1+ yet—the bishop at c3 covers e1. There's nothing in Qe2+ —Black can interpose his queen. Can I bring more pieces into action, as I had hoped when making the castling move? Rb1—the rook would be on an open file, but it doesn't seem to be attacking or moving to anywhere important. White has sacrificed two pawns for attacking hopes.

Third question: What to do? Direction needed and a decision wanted. Do we have to save the rook on a1? Can we get Black's bishop off the diagonal a5–e1? Black's bishop at c3 is loose (i.e. not protected). Can advantage be taken of that? White can play 10 B×f7+ K×f7 11 Qb3+ ; White would regain one of the sacrificed pawns and make Black's king something of a target. It's worth playing.

Fourth question: Have I a better move? When you learn to ask yourself this question, you have an essential ingredient for becoming a good player. Better moves are missed all the time because this question is not asked often enough. In order to try to stop himself from moving too quickly, the great German player, Dr. Siegbert Tarrasch, used to sit on his hands. Have I a better move? Take another look at the whole position on the chessboard. Does it matter if Black takes the rook? He would be putting his bishop out of play. Then I could play Re1+. Black could answer the check with . . . Ke8– f8 or . . . Nc6–e7. What could I usefully do in the meantime? If the brain connects the two squares (e7 and f8), which Black could use in order to defend himself against White's Re1+, I might find the move Bc1–a3. Then if Black continues . . . B×a1 White would win Black's queen by 11 Re1+ Ne7 12 B×e7—when this line is calculated completely out we'll find that material will be approximately equal, but that White's pieces are more active.

Fifth question: Is the intended move safe? Am I being stupid? This question is designed to make one take a last look at the position before moving, but it must be accompanied by a change in perspective. The mind can tackle very involved problems and, at the same time, completely overlook something simple. The number of blunders and oversights can be radically reduced through asking this question. Having made up your mind what to play, you shut off all the work that you've done on the position and then, you eye the position again in a different light.

Continuing the Game

White played **10 Bc1–a3!** If 10 . . . Bc3×a1 11 Rf1—e1+ Nc6–e7 12 Ba3×e7 Qd8×e7 13 Re1×e7+ Ke8×e7 14 Qd1×a1. The position, for the moment, is stabilised. How do we assess this position? A material count would show: White: queen—9–10 points, bishop and knight each just over 3 points—say 16 points for the pieces and 5 for the pawns—total 21; Black: 2 rooks—10 points, bishop 3+, 7 for the pawns—total 20 and a bit points. There is not much between the two sides. White's slight edge is certainly not enough to ensure him of a win. But an 'activity count' shows a definite plus for the white pieces; the two factors combine—very slight material plus together with superior mobility means that White has a clear advantage —not clearly a win but everything to play for.

The game continued **10 . . . d7–d6**. The main alternative is 10 . . . d7–d5. **11 Ra1–c1** (after asking the questions) **11 . . . Bc3–a5** (diag 213). It looks as if Black wants to castle, bring his other pieces into play and remain two pawns up. Where can White attack? Black's bishop on a5 still stops Re1+. This bishop is protected by the knight at c6. White can drive the knight away by 12 d5 (say 12 . . . Ne7) and then fork Black's king and bishop by 13 Qa4+; but Black defends both threats with 13 . . . c6, enabling the queen to protect the bishop. Can White improve on this? Can he play a similar attack using a different order of moves? White played **12 Qd1–a4**. White threatens 13 d5 to take advantage of the pin on the diagonal a4–e8, as well as trying to drive away the bishop's protector. Black rejected the moves

213
W

. . . 0–0 and . . . Bd7 and replied **12 . . . a7–a6**. He wants to play . . . b5 forking White's queen and bishop. White decided that Black would gain sufficient counterplay after 13 d5 b5 and looked for a better move. He played **13 Bc4–d5**. This threatens to take Black's knight with check, thus winning the bishop; 13 . . . b5 would be met by 14 B×c6+ winning two pieces.

Black played **13 . . . Ba5–b6**. White can now consider Re1+. But there are also interesting complications if he should capture on c6, e.g. 14 B×c6+ b×c6 15 Q×c6+ at the same time attacking a black rook; but Black can defend himself with 15 . . . Bd7 and the rook is protected. Pity that White does not still have this bishop at d5 as then he could afford to take the rook. How about if he had initially taken on c6 with the rook instead of the bishop? The game could go 14 . . . b×c6 15 Q×c6+ Bd7 16 Q×a8. White played **14 Rc1×c6** and Black answered **14 . . . Bc8–d7**. White hadn't expected that. He hadn't given the last look round the position before taking the knight! The rook is pinned and cannot retreat.

Trouble

White is in trouble. Black will be able to recapture on c6 at his leisure and White will have lost the equivalent of two more pawns. What to do?

When something unexpected happens on the chessboard, you should allow yourself time to recover from the shock condition. There are varying degrees of shock; most players are susceptible; it is not easily diagnosed; but first reactions are suspect. When surprised, you mustn't immediately react with a counter move. Don't try to convince the opponent that you were waiting for his move! Just allow time for the body and mind to re-adjust; let there be time for the normal chemical constituents of the blood stream to be restored. Many terrible blunders are made under shocked circumstances, moves which are incomprehensible when looked at afterwards. Examine the position calmly.

White can stop Black from castling. Is there better? What can be got for the rook? If 15 R×d6 B×a4 White has 16 R×d8+ but after 16 . . . K×d8 seems to the equivalent of three pawns down without concrete attacking prospects. That would be almost hopeless. But White, determined not to

Finishing the Game

After further analysis and rechecking, White played **15 Rc6×d6** and the game continued **15 . . . c7×d6 16 Rf1–e1+ Ke8–f8 17 Ba3×d6+ Kf8–g8**. The king has no flight square. **18 Nf3–g5! g7–g6!** 18 . . . Q×g5 19 Q×d7 threatens many mates. **19 Ng5×f7 Qd8–c8 20 Nf7–d8+ Kg8–g7 21 Re1–e7+ Kg7–f6 22 Re7–f7+ Kf6–g5 23 Bd6–f4+ Kg5–h5 24 Rf7–d7** White is ahead materially while the black king is in a mating net. The game was wound up by **24 . . . Bb6×d8 25 Qa4–d1+ Kh5–h4 26 g2–g3+ Kh4–h3 27 Bd5–g2** checkmate.

The Five Questions

The lesson of this section is about the five questions that need to be asked before making each move. They are:

1. What's he/she trying to do?
2. How does it affect my plan?
3. What to do?
4. Have I better?
5. Have I the position in perspective?

Some of the procedures and questions asked can be acquired by experience, but training in these methods can mean that your use of them is more economical and effective; they could also provide a basis for increasing one's capacity for thinking. Further, a logical chess training can prevent the development of sloppy thinking methods such as permanently handicap many players.

General Advice

Learn the questions, and improve the form of the questions, that provide information for your thinking centres.

Play through good grandmaster games, that are annotated in reasonable depth, in order to acquire ideas and have models for cohesive chains of thought.

lose, rechecks his calculations. After 15 R×d6 . . . 15 . . . B×a4 . . . White can sandwich in the check 16 Re1+. Black goes 16 . . . Kf8 and then 17 R×d8 is check—no, even better, it is checkmate because it is double check. Now take it coolly. Players often blunder when they are excited. Once more 15 R×d6 B×a4 16 Re1+—Black has an alternative. He can play 16 . . . Qe7. Analysing further, we reach after 17 R×e7+ K×e7 18 R×b6+ a position where White will have won a bishop and knight for a rook—material advantage.

MISTAKES AND BLUNDERS

How and why are mistakes made? A coolly detached diagnosis in this direction plus the determined application of corrections can make a tremendous advance in one's results possible. Great players make many minor errors of judgement but their tremendous will, and perhaps further factors, makes them nearly free of gross blunders.

The reasons for errors and blunders include the following:

Errors are made through *moving too quickly*, for a variety of reasons; when using clocks in serious tournament and match play this may come about through shortage of time.

Errors and gross blunders come about through *fatigue* and *poor physical condition*. An example of fatigue occurred in the 1974 open tournament at Las Palmas (diag 214). Black, in a winning position, played without calculation 1 ... c5×d4?? completely oblivious to the freedom suddenly acquired by White's c-pawn and that it could queen first; he actually sat back in his chair looking very contented.

In the Las Palmas game, fatigue was the main issue, but there was another factor. Krogius, the Russians' specialist chess psychologist, writes that, in appraising a position, there is a tendency and danger to transfer part of a past or passing position to a new situation. Black, having accepted the immovable feature of White's c-pawn for most of the game, in his mind carried that impression on to the position that would result after 1 ... cd.

As an example of this *retained image* Krogius cites the game Ilyin–Zhenevsky v. Nenarokov (diag 215). Note that the black king's position at e8 and where it might seek sanctuary. Ilyin–Zhenevsky calculated the variation 1 Bf7+ Kf8 2 Qh6+ K×f7 3 Rf6+ Ke8 4 Qf8+ Kd7 5 Qg7+ K back 6 Rf8 mating—a neat finish. But what happened? The game went 1 Bf7+ Kf8 2 Qh6+ K×f7 3 Rf6+ and Black played 3 ... Kg8! and gained the advantage. Why—wrote Ilyin–Zhenevsky—should I have overlooked such an obvious move as 3 ... Kg8? The answer is in the position diagrammed; White strongly covers the g8 square with his queen and bishop; it's a most improbable haven for the black king; it was not considered.

Generally players tend to *look at sectors* or parts of the board and very rarely at the board or position as a whole. This can lead to oversights.

214
B

215
W

Before making a move it is a useful habit to make a sweep of the entire board.

Relaxation is the cause of many blunders, and there are many ways in which relaxation comes about, such as sagging from tiredness, taking refreshment, outside distractions and conversations. A typical form, when winning, is to bask in the admiring glances of friends or consterned looks of rivals, or to start to count one's chickens before they are hatched by thinking about the effects of winning on one's rating or prospects. If one relaxes, don't move quickly; wait for some tension and purposefulness to creep back into one's frame.

Changes in the position, like suddenly becoming aware that one is winning, can lead to *nervousness* and want of confidence. Time may be needed in order to re-adjust one-self. The further problem, rigidity of outlook, can lead to the missing of many opportunities.

When something suddenly goes wrong through any of the listed circumstances one can become shocked. *Shock* is a common problem that is not readily diagnosed. Yet if you move quickly in that condition you can make the most incredible blunders. If something unpleasant happens unexpectedly, suspect shock and warped thinking and take your time—some minutes—to recover. Diagram 216 is from a world championship qualifying tournament in 1964. The Hungarian grandmaster, Lengyel, played the bad 41 ... R6×e2+. His opponent (Darga of West Berlin) must have had sudden visions that after 42 R×e2 B×h4+ his king would have to go to g2 and he would lose a rook; therefore he immediately resigned! When

216
B

shown that he had 43 Ke3 with winning chances, all he could do was clap his hands to his head. Both players must have retained the image that e3 was not available to White's king because of the effect from the black rook at e6.

An exciting game is rarely blunder free. Excitement can lead to lack of caution. While you are winning against a stronger or more famous player is the time for utter calm—it's better to enjoy the win afterwards.

Time Pressure

Many games are decided by mistakes in time-trouble. It is quite common for players to leave themselves very little time within which to make many moves. This will require high speed thinking and decision taking from them. Experts can move at a rate of about one move per second and maintain a fairly high standard of play, but this requires an even rhythm of play by the opponent and little tension within the position.

Tendencies of those in time pressure include:

1 the adoption of forcing lines,
2 simplifying,
3 choosing tactical solutions and abandoning long range planning,
4 adoption of non-committal and relatively passive continuations, and
5 over-rating merits of opponent's active opportunities.

In addition to shock and other error factors, some players in serious time pressure become hypnotised by the movement of the clock or spend much of their time nervously glancing at it.

If you are in time trouble and you are stuck for a plan, Len Barden recommends you improve your worst placed piece.

Nikolai Krogius, Spassky's psychological second, wrote that there is no place for great startling discoveries while in extreme time pressure—the important thing is to succeed in making moves that are not bad.

To speed up one's own moves against an opponent in time trouble would be ill-advised; it's better to work out multi-move plans or even to forget about the time-trouble and play to one's own schedule.

Can one be cured of the fault of being habitually in time-trouble? Some people enjoy the excitement and it is doubtful if any treatment will help.

A serious method is to set yourself subsidiary time controls, say 10 moves in 25 minutes, 16 in 65 minutes, 24 in 105, 32 in 135 minutes and 40 in 2½ hours, or even more seriously play special training games in which you have to adhere to the subsidiary time controls at all costs, the quality of play being a secondary consideration. Somehow you must get into yourself that unpleasant decisions or even ordinary decisions must be made without taking long, without seeking much of improbabilities and without striving for absolute perfection.

There are other approaches to trying to curb undisciplined handling of the allocated time. Great players go through an impressive amount of work in a limited time. Of course their experienced first glance will eliminate most of the implausible possibilities. But this means that they can direct a very intensive search of the valid possibilities. Then they try to check the calculation of a variation only once and avoid a common sloppy habit of going over and over an endless treadmill of a variation hoping that something will turn up. I recommend checking calculations no more than twice.

One way of increasing one's work ratio is to play clock games with fast time limits such as five minutes each! It is important when playing such quick games to take them very seriously and to use them for testing ideas and if one is getting into a slap-happy or punch-drunk state to bring a session of such play to a rapid halt.

Endings

Many players wilfully neglect the endings, completely oblivious to the extra confidence that one can play with if one is prepared to play into and not avoid endings. Endings are principally about the promotion of pawns. The general rule applicable to other stages of the game—use your pieces actively —can in the endings be supplemented by the important one of using your king aggressively. Rooks are placed behind both your own advancing pawns on the way to queening and your opponent's similarly advancing passed pawns.

If you are pawns up, tend to exchange the back row pieces and not pawns. Advance passed pawns as quickly as reasonably possible, covering umbrella permitting!

Self-Assessment

Many of us dream of playing fiery attacking games with all the controlled ferocity of an Alekhine or a Tal. They look at attacking moves when they first look at the position. They have an instant awareness of the tactical possibilities. How can one get at the throat of the opponent's position? The great attacking player must in addition have a creative flair for new twists in the opening.

What sort of move do we produce at a time of crisis? Attacking? Non-committal? Counter-attacking? Balanced? Passive? Defensive? Positionally strengthening? What sort of move is the first one we look at? Which tendency triumphs if we look long and hard at the position? The opening we choose should depend on the answer to these questions.

Look at the position in diag 217. You have the black pieces. Your opponent has two more pawns than you and his bishop (c6) is threatening to take your rook (a8) and follow up with d4 and 0–0. What is your first reaction? What would be your considered reply? Turn to p. 92 for discussion.

Seeing Ahead

How far one can see ahead is a favourite talking point. In some positions the answer can be—none for certain. In others, especially when there is a forced variation without branches, the answer can be a large number chess-wise. An experienced chessplayer develops islands of knowledge, each island being a particular type of position about which he has certain judgements. A sample type—'Black has a bad bishop and therefore has an inferior position.' Calculation can be limited to charting a course between such islands.

Another way to see ahead is, in one's mind, to shift the pieces to ideal squares and then to work backwards and forwards to see if the ideal can be achieved. Have a look at the position in diagram 218. The black pieces are curiously constricted. Note that after 1 . . . Kb2 the black pieces are stalemated. White would like to win and even to give an early mate.

What mating position can be visualised? At the moment the black king is in check to the bishop. If the white rook (c6) stood instead at b3 then Black would be double checked and mated. Can such a position be constructed?

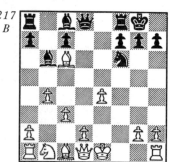

217
B

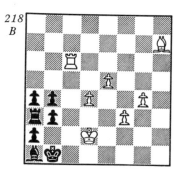

218
B

The rook would have had to move from d3 and take on b3 to give the double check. What was Black's previous move to that? Kb2–b1! How did it get to b2? White's rook somewhere else uncovered the bishop to give check—Re4–e3+. From the final position we can work our way back. The complete solution has one extra twist in that after 1 . . . Kb2 the stalemate is released by 2 Rg6 allowing 2 . . . Kb1; then White can check on alternative moves, by 3 Rf6+ Kb2 4 Rf5 Kb1 5 Rf4+ Kb2 6 Re4 Kb1 7 Re3+ Kb2 8 Rd3 Kb1 9 R×b3++ mate. White, by visualising the end position, has been enabled to see eight moves ahead.

A GAME AT CHESS WITH LIVING PIECES, AT HEIGHINGTON, NEAR DARLINGTON.

6 Planning your openings

Opening Knowledge

The most feared aspect of modern chess is knowledge. There is a huge outpouring of specialist opening books (see p. 92 for a list of Batsford's Contemporary Chess Openings series), books giving the games of important current events and periodicals. For instance, the Nottingham-based periodical *The Chess Player* gives annually about 2500 games, mostly with notes, and the twice-yearly Yugoslav publication *Chess Informator* has 1400–1500. To try to keep up to date seems an impossible labour.

One wants results to depend on ability at, and understanding of, chess. Nobody wants to lose to, or be saddled with a manifestly inferior game by, an opponent who has simply memorised a great number of grandmaster games, and particularly if you think you are superior in most other aspects. And most players can't afford to give up their job to study all the available material, though they don't want to be outside the current thinking and ideas about chess.

Only young people have a memory storage capacity sufficient to cope with the quantity of games that it may be useful to know. Older people need to try and formulate guide rules and what are called principles to help them. Neither method is completely self-sufficient.

All players, young and old, should play through some master games in their entirety. One remembers games and the associated opening better.

It is normal for players to specialise in a limited range of openings and to acquire a knowledge within the selected repertoire. The procedure would work out thus.

You would decide, stage 1 which opening to play as White. 2: list the systems with which your opponents are likely to reply, and 3: prepare the outline of a plan against each system. When preparing for playing as Black, you come in at stage 2 and add stage 4, the preparation of specific variations against stage 3. But first, what is one trying to do at the beginning of the game?

Opening Aims

One aims to bring the back row pieces to squares and lines where they will strongly influenced the course of play. One tries at the same time to frustrate the opponent's efforts to do the same. These aims remain the same throughout the game.

If there is no specific target, take the trouble to improve the scope of each piece. Give some thought as to where they will stand best. For example: put a knight in the corner of an empty board (diag 219). The circles show the squares to which the piece can go. There are only two (f2 and g3), but if the knight is further up the board its range increases to three and four (diags 220 and 221). The circles in diagram 222 show that on g3 (or any other post on the second frame—squares g2–g7–b7–b2–g2) the knight commands six squares, and on any of the sixteen inner squares of the chessboard (f3–f6–c6–c3–f3), e.g. f3, (diag 223), there's a choice of eight squares immediately available. A knight takes time to hop from one wing to the other—from a central square it's not far to any outer square.

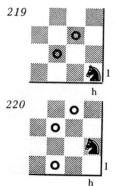

219

220

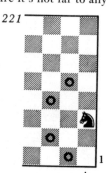

221

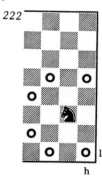

222

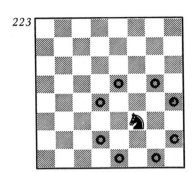

223

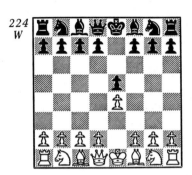

224
W

In actual play the board is cluttered with obstacles from one's own pieces and dangers from the opponent's; opposing pawns can be set to act as mine-fields. But generally the aim is to bring knights into, and operate them from, the central squares.

Bishops have a similar increase in scope. From the outer ring they might go to seven squares; the next ring in could add the number to nine, and so on. In the central four squares (e4/e5/d5/d4) the total could be thirteen. The rule is—operate knights and bishops towards and from the centre.

Rooks are very different. Wherever they stand on the board they can go to a maximum of fourteen squares. In fact the rooks operate best at long range. Being in the centre can be an embarrassment to them. Rooks are best stationed on open files, to await the exchange of the minor pieces—knights and bishops—before penetrating into enemy territory.

It's difficult to lay down firm rules for the queen. Lone raids are generally frowned on. She is at her best as a co-operative piece. Fixed placing is a rarity. Even early centralisation has its drawbacks—because of her high value, she can attract and help the opponent's pieces to better squares. My advice is—keep the queen in readiness to co-operate with your other pieces.

The king is normally kept safely out of the way of its own and opposition pieces until the later stages of the game. In the endings it can be vigorously used.

Pawns are moved for four reasons:
1 to free one's own pieces;
2 to be exchanged, and thus create either open files for the rooks or other ways of breaching the enemy's position;
3 to be promoted;
4 to restrict the opponent's activity.

As White starts, the initial struggle can readily be between White having one more piece active and Black, after his move, just managing to keep level. This particular aspect is noticeable most in positions where similar central pawn moves are made such as 1 e4 e5 2 Nf3 Nc6 3 d4. This factor is responsible for the statistics of a much greater number of wins for the white pieces.

If you have a choice between which piece to move, it is a good rule to play the one that has the least number of options. In the position after 1 e4 e5 (diag 224), the knight on g1 has one main route to the centre (via f3 to e5) while the bishop on f1 has—as our experience tells us—posts both at c4 and at b5. Therefore most people prefer to play 2 Ng1-f3 rather than to move the bishop. This is the theorising behind the general instruction of 'knights before bishops'; of course there are plenty of exceptions to the rule.

Summarising this information, we can plan our power set-up. Knights and bishops are to function across the central squares. Rooks will need open files which may necessitate an exchange of pawns. The queen will be kept at the ready but off the back row out of the way of the rooks. The king is to be tucked safely away.

Harmonious Development
The next step, which should be self-evident, is that we should dispose our pieces and pawns in such a manner that they work in harmony together. They should not only stand well individually but should work as a team. The side that has the best in both factors must have the better chances of winning.

Let us look at a good example of harmonious development by White. **1 e4 e5 2 Bc4 Nf6 3 d3.** This opens a way for the other bishop. **3 . . . Bc5 4 Nc3 d6 5 f4** White is preparing a file for his rook at h1, as after White has

castled his rook will be posted actively on f1. **5 ... Nc6 6 Nf3 Bg4 7 Na4**
This is to eliminate the black bishop on the c5–g1 diagonal; it's holding up
White's castling. **7 ... Bb6 8 h3 B×f3 9 Q×f3 Nd4 10 Qf2** (diag 225).
Now White is ready to continue with such moves as N×b6, c3, 0–0, Be3
and Rael satisfactorily completed the first stage of the opening – his immediate mobilisation. Before him, however, stretches a long continual
struggle to improve the position of his pieces until they completely dominate
the board. And this is where factors like stamina, will and determination
play their part.

The depth to which you prepare your repertoire must depend on two
factors, the calibre of the opposition and the standard reached in one's own
play.

Beginner's Plan

If you are a beginner you may be plagued by opponents who keep trying to
inflict the four move checkmate (1 e4, 2 Bc4, 3 Qh5 and 4 Q×f7) on you.
You can begin to cure them by answering move **1 e2–e4** with **1 ... e7–e6**—
just one square—and when they persist with 2 Bf1–c4 to attack it by 2 ...
d7–d5; your d5 pawn is supported by the e-pawn and the queen. If White
takes (3 e4×d5), you recapture by 3 ... e6×d5. The white bishop's diagonal
c4–f7 has been blocked off and you can keep it blocked.

When, after 1 e2–e4 e7–e6 White tries to vary the approach by playing
2 Qd1–h5, the queen can be driven away by 2 ... Ng8–f6 and then next
move perhaps play 3 ... d7–d5. When White varies once more by 2 Qd1–
f3 play 2...d7–d5. Indeed you can safely answer practically every method of
White's by the two moves 1 ... e7–e6 and 2 ... d7–d5.

Simple Repertoire

Here as a sample is a very simple form of Black repertoire, with a plan to
answer each important White opening. When Black, you meet:

1 e4 with 1 ... e5
1 d4 with 1 ... d5
1 Nf3 with 1 ... d5
1 c4 with 1 ... e5

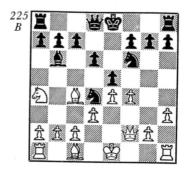

225
B

Against odd moves like 1 b3 there's 1 ... e5 and against 1 g3, also 1 ... e5;
even if 1 f4, 1 ... e5 is a good reply. In other words—when it's safe to play
... e5 you do so; otherwise you fall back on ... d5.

As White plays 1 e4. It's not a bad repertoire.

When you have decided on your repertoire, keep refreshing it by playing
through the moves of relevant games published in newspaper columns or
the more specialist sources. You should make a habit of playing through the
entire moves of these games; that way a greater impact is made on your
memory and besides you are likely to add to your general understanding.

Universal Repertoires for Black

If you have very restricted time for study you'll be tempted to base your defence on a universal system applicable against any opening that White can
come up with; then one confines one's study to the formations and conditions that will force you to modify your system.

The first universal system that comes to mind is one that extends the
Beginners Plan. Black plays **1 ... e6** and **2 ... d5** against practically every
set-up that White can adopt. This may be followed by ... c5, with the
knight at g8 going to e7 or f6 and the other knight (b8) usually being developed at c6. The bishop f8 can go to e7 or d6 or c5 or b4 depending on
circumstances. There may be problems with the other bishop, but these
are not insoluble; it could be fianchettoed by ... b6 and ... Bb7. In any
repertoire as Black, it is impossible to lay down the files that should be

opened or fought over for the rooks—which files will depend on how White disposes his pawns. But this opening (1 . . . e6 followed by 2 . . . d5) establishes the basis for a solid, sound position.

The reversed system with the centre pawns (1 . . . d6 and 2 . . . e5) is a possibility; but White can complicate its set-up after 1 d4 d6 by playing 2 Nf3; Black will need to prepare the . . . e5 move by . . . Nbd7 or . . . Nc6 or by getting rid of White's knight by 2 . . . Bg4 and later exchanging it.

Universal with . . . c6 and . . . d5
A third universal system of defence for Black is the combination **1 . . . c6** followed by **2 . . . d5**. 1 e4 c6 2 d4 d5 is the Caro-Kann Defence and 1 d4 c6 2 c4 d5 is the Slav Defence. In both defences Black keeps open the c8–h3 diagonal for developing his c8-bishop.

Modern Universal Systems
The universal system that is currently interesting the world's leading players is based on the moves . . . **g6** followed by . . . **Bg7** together with . . . **d6** with diagonals open for both bishops. It may not matter which Black plays first, 1 . . . g6 or 1 . . . d6. In due time the d6 pawn supports advances like c7–c5 and . . . e7–e5, while Black's pawn formation is elastic enough to contemplate such additions as . . . c7–c6, . . . a7–a6 and . . . b7–b5 or . . . b7–b6. Even this re-arrangement . . . c7–c6 and . . . d6–d5 or the early advance . . . f7–f5 could be feasible.

These systems of defence are covered by Ray Keene and George Botter-

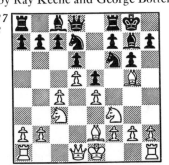

226
W

227
B

ill's books *The Pirc Defence* and *The Modern Defence*, supplemented by another Batsford book *The King's Indian Defence*, written by three British champions, Ray Keene, Bill Hartston and Len Barden.

In this modern system, the knight g8 usually comes to f6, but there are a few odd lines where the knight travels via e7 or h6. One must be even less dogmatic about the development of the other black pieces, but then, the whittling away of dogma is a characteristic of our age.

King's Indian Defence
If White adopts the order **1 d4 g6 2 c4 d6 3 Nc3 Bg7 4 e4** Black can revert to the well-known King's Indian Defence lines with knight out **4 . . . Nf6** (diag 226).

Against the Sämisch system (**5 f3**) a very up-to-date combative idea is **5 . . . Nc6 6 Be3** and now, as his position is not under pressure, Black can prepare by **6 . . . a6 7 Nge2 Rb8** to open a file on the queen's wing; a 1971 Russian game continued **8 Nc1 e5 9 d5 Nd4** White could now win a pawn by 10 B×d4 ed 11 Q×d4, but Black would obtain plenty of counterplay after 11 . . . 0–0. **10 N1e2 c5 11 dc** en passant **bc 12 N×d4 ed 13 B×d4 R×b2** Now, when White mistakenly tried to exploit the situation of the intruding rook by **14 Nb5**, Black hit back hard with **14 . . . N×e4!** After **15 B×b2 Qa5+ 16 Nc3 B×c3+ 17 B×c3 Q×c3+ 18 Ke2 Be6**, with its further threats to the white king, brought about White's acknowledgement of defeat.

These moves worked well for Black against the Sämisch set-up (f3, Be3 and Nge2 for White), but would not necessarily do against other plans. White could play, from diagram 226, **5 Be2 0–0 6 Nf3 e5**. This is an important point of divergences.

Petrosian's plan 7 d5 Nbd7 8 Bg5 (diag 227), is met by K-side manoeuvres (8 . . . h6 9 Bh4 g5 10 Bg3 Nh5) when, as compensation for the weakening of his king's side, Black can hope to play . . . f5 and have the better placed pieces.

Yet another system for White arises from the moves 7 0–0 Nc6 8 d5; after 8 . . . Ne7 Black can aim to play . . . Nd7 (or even . . . Ne8), followed by . . . f5.

If White sets up a massive pawn centre by **5 f4 0–0 6 Nf3**, Black can challenge it with 6 . . . c5 (diag 228), and if 7 d5 continue to chivy it with 7 . . . e6.

Against another popular White plan of development, **4 g3 Nf6 5 Bg2 0–0 6 Nc3**, can be commended the system 6 . . . Nc6 7 0–0 Bf5 used by Fischer against Petrosian in 1966.

One cannot over-emphasise that, in setting up a framework of openings, you must fill in that frame with a knowledge gained from playing through games using these openings right to the last move. These variations, six, seven or even ten moves long, are hopelessly inadequate in themselves.

Pirc Defence

If White starts **1 e4 d6 2 d4** Black could well interpose 2 . . . **Nf6** immediately—it cuts down White's possibilities—and then on **3 Nc3** to continue 3 . . . **g6** (diag 229). White has several possible plans here. 4 f4 Bg7 Nf3 is the popular Austrian Attack. After 5 . . . 0–0 it can take several forms: one is 6 e5 Nfd7; another 6 Be2 c5 7 dc Qa5 (threatening . . . N × e4) and a third way is 6 Bd3 Nc6.

A more solid continuation for White is 4 Nf3 Bg7 5 Be2 0–0 6 0–0 when Black can try 6 . . . Bg4 or, with a similar objective, 6 . . . Nc6.

Black has to treat White's plan 4 Bc4 Bg7 5 Qe2 with extreme care. This sharp variation was recommended to round off your repertoire when you're White, p. 72. Perhaps best is 5 . . . c6.

Avoid routine thinking even if you adopt a universal defence. In postal chess players try to cut down on postage and time by sending 'conditional' moves; for instance they are used for obvious recaptures. In one particular game, White posted off his score sheet 1 d4. What happened was told by the player who had Black. He saved a lot of postage by replying 1 . . . g6 and pencilled in the conditional 'any', meaning any move by White, 2 . . . Bg7. When the score-sheet came back inked in 2 Bh6 Bg7 3 B × g7, he, having lost a bishop, and faced with the loss of a rook, gracefully resigned.

Benoni or Benko Gambit

There's another defence that could well be built into a repertoire for Black. This is the Benoni Gambit (or as the Americans call it, the Benko Gambit) against the Queen's Pawn Opening. It goes **1 d4 Nf6 2 c4 c5 3 d5 b5 4 cb a6 5 ba B × a6** (diag 230). Black wants to have pressure along the two open files and to use that as a way of turning White's position. Black would envisage a position something like diagram 231. See the co-ordination between the rook at b8 and the fianchettoed bishop at g7 against White's b2 pawn; that could hold up the development of White's bishop at c1 and the rook a1. The black knight f6 is no fixture; the other knight at d7—one imagines a possible post at d3, realised by . . . c4 and . . . Nc5; other plans for the knight include going via d7 and b6 to c4 or a4, or even the journey Nb8–a6–c7–b5–d4. The queen usually has no fixed post—it could be placed on any of a5, b6 or c7. That's a good jumping off position for the pieces. I think the gambit is very good. I've no qualms about playing it.

But what is a suitable opening for a similar attitude if White plays 1 e4? In queen side operations from the Benoni Gambit, the black king position is not at high risk, but gambits on the other wing (like e4 e5 2 Nf3 f5!?) particularly expose the king. Black's best counter-attacking defence is generally thought to be the Sicilian.

One can play the Sicilian with **1 e4 c5 2 Nf3** then 2 . . . **g6**. If White plays the normal sort of plan (3 d4) Black could continue development and pressure (3 . . . Bg7) as 4 dc can be coped with by 4 . . . Qa5+.

Or you could try to master the Sicilian Dragon Variation: **1 e4 c5 2 Nf3 d6 3 d4 cd 4 N × d4 Nf6 5 Nc3 g6**. It's a lot of work, but you could find it worthwhile to study David Levy's book *The Sicilian Dragon* (Batsford).

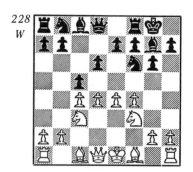

228
W

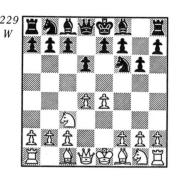

229
W

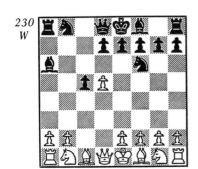

230
W

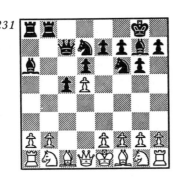

231

WHEN WHITE—(A Serious Repertoire)

Let's imagine you are preparing openings for very serious competitions. When White, you decide to continue with 1 e4 which you think fits your image. Nowadays you expect to meet 1 . . . e5 or 1 . . . c5 most often. You'll need therefore to study them in some depth. Less usual moves are: 1 . . . g6; 1 . . . d6; 1 . . . Nf6; 1 . . . e6; 1 . . . d5; 1 . . . c6 and even 1 . . . Nc6; they will all require some attention.

The King's Gambit

After **1 e4 e5** I strongly want to recommend the King's Gambit **2 f4** (diag 232).

It's an ancient opening which has not been very popular. But I estimate that it is due for a revival. Among those who have played it in recent years are Spassky, Bronstein, Korchnoi, Keres, Planinc, Basman. . . . Fischer made a determined effort in 1960–61 to refute the opening before adopting it himself. White sacrifices a pawn to free the centre for his own pawns and pieces. There is a prospect for early castling and targets for the rook along the f-file. It has the additional psychological advantage that lots of opponents will underestimate its true qualities through the years of neglect. The opening leads to lively yet unclear positions in which White has as prolonged an initiative as in the move popular Ruy Lopez (1 e4 e5 2 Nf3 Nc6 3 Bb5). For detailed study I would refer readers to the book *The King's Gambit* by Victor Korchnoi and Vladimir Zak (Batsford). Their work contains many new ideas and appreciations.

I am giving you an expert repertoire based on the King's Gambit. **1 e4 e5 2 f4**. Black can reply 2 . . . ef (accepting the gambit pawn); 2 . . . d5!? (Falkbeer's Counter-Gambit); 2 . . . Nf6 and 2 . . . Qh4+ —both counter-attacking; and decline the gambit with 2 . . . Bc5 and 2 . . . d6. Some details on each line follows.

KING'S GAMBIT ACCEPTED

After **2 . . . ef3 Nf3!** Black has a) 3 . . . g5, b) 3 . . . h6, c 3 . . . d6, d) 3 . . . Nf6, e) 3 . . . d5 and f) 3 . . . Be7.

a) **3 . . . g5 4 h4 g4 5 Ne5!**

This is the Kieseritsky Gambit. Akiba Rubinstein, one of the greatest

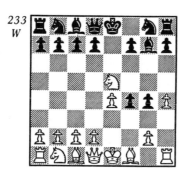

positional players of the early years of this century, spent years analysing the complications of this variation in the belief that White should win. His judgment seems sound.

5 . . . Bg7! (diag 233) From a wide choice, which include 5 . . . d5, 5 . . . Nf6 and 5 . . . h5, this is probably best.

6 d4 Nf6 7 Nc3 d6 8 Nd3 0–0 9 N×f4 N×e4 10 N×e4 Re8 11 Kf2 R×e4 12 c3 Qf6! Not prepared to retreat 13 g3 Bh6 14 Bd3 B×f4 15 B×f4 R×f4+ 16 gf Q×f4+ 17 Ke2!! g3 18 Qd2! Bg4+ 19 Ke1 with a tense position which should go in White's favour as Black's knight and rook are still out of play, e.g. 19 . . . Qf3 20 Rf1 g2 21 R×f3 g1=Q+ 22 Rf1.

If you obtain a game which leads into this particular variation, don't expect it will follow automatically through to move 22. Therefore study each move and try to determine the reasons for it being played and wherein lay the choice. Play through Kieseritsky Gambit games as you find them and add their ideas to your background knowledge.

Never accept the recommended moves of opening books as complete gospel. Their lines are being constantly subjected to change and improvement.

b) 3 . . . h6
4 d4 g5 5 h4 Bg7 6 g3 g4 7 Nh2 fg 8 N×g4 d6 9 c3 Nf6 10 N×f6+ Q×f6 11 Be3 Nc6 12 Nd2 Bd7 13 Qb3 0–0–0 14 0–0–0.

Though White remains a pawn down, his pieces are very active. This more than compensates him for the material deficit.

c) 3 . . . d6
Bobby Fischer's line. He tried to refute the King's Gambit with this move in 1961. His follow-up enables Black to avoid the Kieseritsky and other conventional ideas. However, White can play a restrained continuation, not analysed in Fischer's article.

4 d3 g5 5 h4 g4 6 Ng1! (diag 234)

Note that White is not dogmatic in his play with this piece. In the Kieseritsky it went to e5, in the second variation it retreated to h2; g1 is a third possibility. In other variations Ng5 is utilised.

6 . . . Bh6 7 Bd2 Nc6 8 Nc3 Be6 9 Nce2! In this case White wins back the pawn with a good game. White's overall plan has been to hold back his centre in order to avoid premature pawn exchanges.

d) 3 . . . Nf6
4 e5 Nh5 5 Qe2 This is played to discourage Black's . . . d6 or . . . d5. 5 . . . Be7 6 d4 0–0 6 . . . Bh4+ would prove a waste of time. 7 Nc3 d6 8 Bd2 de 9 de Bh4+ 10 g3 fg 11 0–0–0 Bd7 12 hg N×g3 13 Qh2. All this happened in a game won by the British master, Michael Basman, a few years ago. White has lots of open lines on to Black's king position.

e) 3 . . . d5
4 ed Nf6 5 Bb5+ 5 Nc3 Bd6 might also turn out a little better for White. 5 . . . c6 6 dc N×c6!? 7 d4 Bd6 8 0–0 This improves upon White's play in the game Hartston–Spassky, from the 1965–66 Hastings tournament. 8 . . . 0–0 9 c3 Bg4 10 Nbd2 Nd5 11 Nc4 Bc7 12 Qd3

White's central control gives him the better of it.

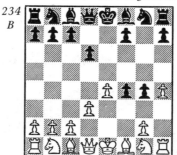

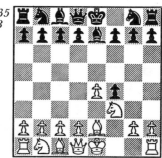

f) **3 . . . Be7**

4 Be2 (diag 235) This is the newest research idea here! **4 . . . Nf6** After 4 . . . Bh4+ 5 Kf1 Be7 it's difficult to know whether White's unhappy king position fully justifies the waste of time. Now 6 d4 g5 7 Ne5 h5 8 Bc4 would give White excellent play. **5 Nc3 d5 6 ed N×d5 7 N×d5 Q×d5 8 d4 g5 9 0–0** and White has lots of attacking chances.

FALKBEER'S COUNTER-GAMBIT

2 . . . d5!? (diag 236)

This is the Falkbeer Counter-Gambit, which tries to show that White's f4 move was wasteful. **3 ed e4!? 4 d3 Nf6 5 de!** Most masters now believe this to be White's best continuation against the Falkbeer. Play could well continue **5 . . . N×e4 6 Nf3 Bc5 7 Qe2 Bf5 8 Nc3 Qe7 9 Be3 B×e3 10 Q×e3 N×c3 11 Q×e7+ K×e7 12 b2×c3** with serious difficulties for Black.

COUNTER-ATTACK BY 2 . . . Nf6 AND 2 . . . Qh4+

2 . . . Nf6

This little known method of defence, which I used in a game with Fischer in 1968, can take a lot of the sting out of the gambit; that game went **3 fe N×e4 4 Nf3 Ng5 5 d4** (White could try 5 c3, with a slower build-up.) **5 . . . N×f3+ 6 Q×f3 Qh4+ 7 Qf2 Q×f2+ 8 K×f2 Nc6 9 c3 d6.**

2 . . . Qh4+!?

3 g3 Qe7 Ray Keene, the 1971 British Champion, has been experimenting with this idea, which is intended to weaken the White king's likely refuge. If 4 fe d6! 5 ed Q×e4+.

GAMBIT DECLINED 2 . . . Bc5 AND 2 . . . d6

2 . . . Bc5!

An old, reliable way of declining the gambit. If now 3 f4×e5, White will find 3 . . . Qh4+ awkward. **3 Nf3 d6 4 Bc4 4 c3** is another plan. **4 . . . Nf6 5 Nc3 Nc6 6 d3** when Black's best move is **6 . . . a6!** (diag 237), to keep the embarrassing bishop that prevents White's 0–0; but White remains with lots of chances.

2 . . . d6

Against this quiet move, White can build up pressure; **3 Nf3 Nf6 4 Nc3 Nc6 5 Bb5 Bd7 6 d3 e5×f4 7 B×f4** with 0–0 to follow, when the rook comes

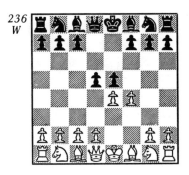

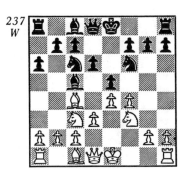

to a good open file.

SPASSKY–BRONSTEIN

As an illustration of the lively character of the King's Gambit, here is the game Spassky–Bronstein, played at Leningrad in 1960: 1 e4 e5 2 f4 ef 3 Nf3 d5 4 ed Bd6 5 Nc3 Ne7 6 d4 0–0 7 Bd3 Nd7 8 0–0 h6?(*8 . . . Ng6 and 8 . . . Nf6 are better.*) 9 Ne4 N×d5 10 c4 Ne3 11 B×e3 fe 12 c5 Be7 13 Bc2! Re8 14 Qd3 e2 15 Nd6! Nf8? (*Leads to a loss. Spassky suggested 15 . . . B×d6, upon which there could follow 16 Qh7+ Kf8 17 cd ef= Q+ 18 R×f1 cd 19 Qh8+ Ke7 20 Re1+ Ne5 21 Q×g7 Rg8 22 Q×h6 Qb6 23 Kh1 Be6 24 de d5, as a possible line of defence.*) 16 N×f7! ef=Q+ 17 R×f1 Bf5 (*If 17 . . . K×f7 18 Ne5++ and mates, or 17 . . . Qd5 18 N3e5 should win.*) 18 Q×f5 Qd7 19 Qf4 Bf6 20 N3e5 Qe7 21 Bb3 B×e5 22 N×e5+ Kh7 23 Qe4+ and Black resigned.

Against the Sicilian

The Sicilian Defence, reached after **1 e4 c5**, is contemporarily the most popular defence to White's king pawn opening. The best way of tackling it is to play into the main variations with 2 Nf3 followed by 3 d4 cd N×d4, but there is a tremendous amount of knowledge that you may feel obliged to acquire.

Therefore against the Sicilian I am recommending that readers adopt the Morra Gambit **2 d4 cd 3 c3** (diag 238). This originated in the last century,

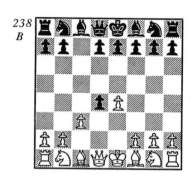

238
B

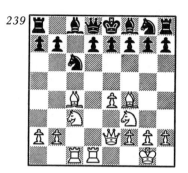

239

was forgotten, and then resuscitated in the 1950's by the Yugoslav grand-master, Milan Matulovic.

White sacrifices a pawn for quick development of the pieces. Matulovic won many short games with it. If Black defends ably and White continues in the correct spirit, Black can obtain at best a position with about level chances. A typical first phase development plan for White after the gambit is accepted (3 . . . dc 4 N×c3) is shown in diagram 239.

After 1 e4 c5 2 d4 dc 3 c3, what replies can Black consider? There is the gambit accepted by 3 . . . dc 4 N×c3, or two important ways of declining—3 . . . Nf6 and 3 . . . d5.

MORRA GAMBIT ACCEPTED

After **1 e4 c5 2 d4 cd 3 c3 dc 4 N×c3 Nc6 5 Nf3** Black has four main plans of development—a) 5 . . . g6 b) 5 . . . e5 c) 5 . . . e6 d) 5 . . . d6.

a)**5 . . . g6**

6 Bc4 Bg7 7 e5! (diag 240)

This disruptive pawn thrust gives White a fierce attack; two samples—7 . . . B×e5 8 B×f7+ K×f7 9 N×e5+ N×e5 10 Qd5+ and takes the knight, unless Black is foolhardy enough to advance his king into gravest danger; after 7 . . . Qa5 8 0–0 N×e5 9 N×e5 B×e5 10 Nd5 f6 11 Re1 is very promising for White—if, say, 11 . . . f6 White plays 12 Bb3 (*threatening 13 f4*) 12 . . . Kf7 13 R×e5 fe 14 Qf3+ Ke8 15 Bh6! N×h6 16 Qf6 when White threatens to mate by 17 Qe7 or take the rook on h8.

b) **5 . . . e5**

6 Bc4 puts Black in grave trouble, e.g. 6 . . . Be7? 7 Qd5 and White has great hopes of a quick win, or 6 . . . Bc5 7 B×f7+.

c) **5 . . . e6**

6 Bc4 a6 7 Qe2 b5 Black plans expansion on the queen's side. However, White can continue with his basic developing plan. **8 Bb3 d6 9 0–0 Be7 10 Rd1 Qc7 11 Bf4 Bb7 12 Rac1 Qb8 13 e5 d5 14 B×d5 ed 15 N×d5** when White threatens 16 e6, with a strong attack.

d) **5 . . . d6**

6 Bc4 (diag 241) **6 . . . e6** This is Black's most stable system.

Black can also try:

1) 6 . . . Nf6?! 7 e5 de (diag 242. *In a game at the 1973 Junior World Championships, Black lost his queen after 7 . . . N×e5?? 8 N× e5 de 9 B×f7+.*) 8 Q×d8+ N×d8 (*Another illustrative game—8 . . . K×d8 9 Ng5 Kc7?! 10 N×f7 Rg8 11 Nb5+ Kb8 12 N×e5 N×e5 13 Bf4 Nfd7 14 B×g8 a6 15 Nd4 Ka7 16 0–0 Black resigned.*) 9 Nb5 Rb8 10 N×e5 e6 11 Nc7+ Ke7 12 Be3 and White threatens 13 Bc5; White's strong initiative, properly exploited, should yield a win.

2) 6 . . . a6 (*as played by two grandmasters at the strong San Antonio, Texas, tournament of 1972; Ken Smith, the American master played—rather routinely—7 0–0. He would have done better to follow a recommendation from Moscow's Central Chess Club bulletin, with . . .*) 7 e5 de (If 7 . . . e6 8 Bg5 8 Q×d8+ N×d8 (Or 8 . . . K×d8 9 Ng5 Nh6 10 B×f7) 9 Nd5! with threats; one line from Moscow leads on from 9 . . . Ne6 10 Nb6 Rb8 11

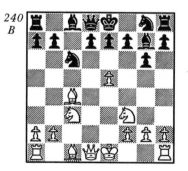

240
B

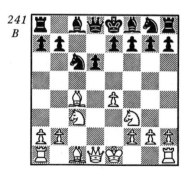

241
B

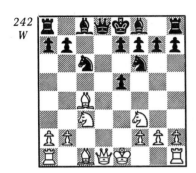

242
W

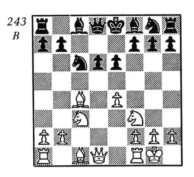

243
B

N × e5 Nf6 to the startling **12 N × f7! K × f7 13 Bf4** with a nice position to have.

7 0–0 (Diag 243) when again I append examples of play:

1) **7 . . . Nge7 8 Bg5 a6** (*If 8 . . . h6 9 Nb5!*) **9 Qe2 h6 10 Be3 Bd7 11 Rad1 Ng6** when White can play **12 Nd4** planning f2–f4–f5.

2) **7 . . . Nf6 8 Qe2 a6 9 Rd1 Qc7 10 Bf4 Ne5 11 B × e5 de 12 Racl Bd7** (*On 12 . . . Qb8 13 Bb5+! gives White a strong attack.*) **13 B × e6 B × e6 14 Nd5 Qb8 15 Nc7+ Ke7 16 Qd2 Ne8 17 N × e6 fe 18 Qd7+ Kf6 19 Ng5 K × g5 20 Q × e6 Nf6 21 Qf5+ Kh6 22 Rc3 Qe8** (*Or 22 . . . Nh5 23 Rh3 g6 24 Rh5 gh 25 Qf6 mate*) **23 Rh3+ Qh5 24 g4 Q × h3 25 g5+ Kh5 26 Q × h3+ K × g5 27 Qf5+ Kh6 28 Rd3 Nh5 29 Rh3 g6 30 R × h5+ Kg7 31 Q × e5** and White's material advantage should enable him to win.

3) **7 . . . Nf6 8 Qe2 Be7 9 Rd1** (Diag. 244. Threat *e5*) **9 . . . e5!** (*Best; if 9 . . . Bd7 10 Bg5 0–0 11 B × f6 gf! 12 Nb5 Qb8 13 Rd3 a6? 14 N × d6! with a continuing initiative.*) **10 h3!** (*White's enduring advantage is through the greater scope of his pieces; it's worthwhile to prevent . . . . Bg4.*) **10 . . . 0–0 11 b3 a6 12 Ba3 Qa5 13 Qb2 Nb4 14 Racl b5 15 B × b4 Q × b4 16 Nd5 N × d5 17 B × d5 Ra7** when White's pieces are much better co-ordinated. Now he can prepare by **18 Rc2** to double on the c-file.

4) **7 . . . a6 8 Qe2 Be7 9 Rd1 Bd7** is an order of moves causing concern at the time of writing. Where is White to develop his c1-bishop? Black has held back from . . . Nf6 in order to avoid White's Bg5. **10 Bf4** would encourage Black to play **10 . . . e5 11 Be3 Bg4** with activity that casts doubts

on the sufficiency of White's pawn sacrifice. Perhaps White should postpone the decision and play **10 h3** and after **10 . . . Nf6 11 Bg5 0–0 12 B × f6 gf!** look into attacking possiblities based on e4–e5 or restraining Black's pieces by **13 a4**.

The position at diagram 245, after **12 . . . gf**, is psychologically interesting. If, on taking the white side of the position, you feel that you are a pawn down and that you are desperately trying to regain it and re-establish a balance, then you should not be playing gambit openings. If, however, you naturally contrast the power and possibilities of the white pieces with those of Black's, and feel that you can make something of it, then you can play this opening.

MORRA GAMBIT DECLINED

After **1 e4 c5 2 d4 cd 3 c3** Black can decline the gambit by **3 . . . Nf6** and **3 . . . d5**, e.g.

3 . . . Nf6

This is the usual reaction from opponents who are suddenly confronted with the Morra Gambit. **4 e5 Nd5 5 Bc4 Qc7!** (If **5 . . . Nb6 6 Bb3** or **5 . . . e6 d4**) **6 Qe2 Nb6 7 Bb3** (Also possible is 7 Bd3.) **7 . . . d3!? 8 Qe4 Na6**

244
B

245
W

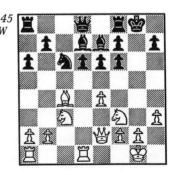

9 Be3 Nc5 10 B × c5 Q × c5 11 Nf3 with White having a reasonable position. Black cannot save his advanced pawn.

      3 . . . d5

when a game played by former champion, Alexander Alekhine, can serve as a model for White

4 ed Q × d5 5 cd Nc6 6 Nf3 Bg4 7 Be2 e6 8 Nc3 Bb4 9 0–0 Qa5 10 a3 (diag 246).

Now Black should play 10 . . . B × c3 11 bc Nf6; instead he gave Alekhine the opportunity to carry out a vigorous attack against the uncastled black king.

      10 . . . Nf6 11 d5!! ed 12 ab! Q × a1 13 Nd2 This threatens to net the black queen by 14 Nb3. **13 . . . B × e2 14 Q × e2+ Ne7 15 Re1 0–0 16 Nb3 Qa6 17 Q × a6 ba 18 R × e7**

White has a material and positional advantage and duly won; Alekhine–Podgorny, Prague 1943.

Other Defences to 1 e2–e4

I give one short line of play as a sample, against each of the less likely defences that you may encounter.

PIRC DEFENCE

After **1 e4 d6 2 d4 Nf6** White could adopt the system 3 Nc3 g6 4 Bc4 Bg7 5 Qe2 as the opening 'theorists' are divided over what is a sufficient reply for Black.

KING'S FIANCHETTO DEFENCE

Against this 'modern' defence **1 e4 g6** White can continue 2 d4 Bg7 3 c3 and later f4.

ALEKHINE'S DEFENCE

Against this (**1 e4 Nf6**) you could try the unusual line 2 e5 Nd5 3 Bc4 Nb6 4 Bb3 d6 5 d4 ed 6 Qh5, threatening mate, but don't be upset if it doesn't come off, you'll still have a reasonable game.

FRENCH DEFENCE

This is **1 e4 e6** (the beginner's plan—see p. 64). I would follow up 2 d4 d5 3 Nc3 and whether my opponent chooses the classical line 3 . . . Nf6 or

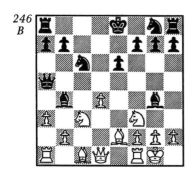

246
B

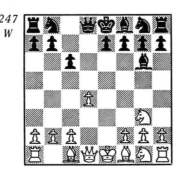

247
W

goes into the knotty Winawer Variation, 3 . . . Bb4, then continue with the straightforward old-fashioned bishop development 4 Bd3.

CENTRE COUNTER

If your opponent should play it (**1 e4 d5**), take the pawn (2 ed); if the queen recaptures (2 . . . Q×d5) White faces no severe opening problems after 3 Nc3 followed by 4 d4. When the recapture, possible on move 2, is delayed by 2 . . . Nf6, don't try to hold on to the pawn but play 3 d4 N×d5 4 Nf3.

CARO–KANN DEFENCE

This (**1 e4 c6**) has been a favourite of three world champions. Though not active in appearance it must not be treated disdainfully. Spassky, when trying to wrest the world championship title from Petrosian used the line 2 d4 d5 3 Nc3 de 4 N×e4 Bf5 5 Ng3 Bg6 (diag 247) 6 h4 h6 7 Nf3 Nd7 8 h5 Bh7 9 Bd3 B×d3 10 Q×d3 Qc7 11 Bd2 e6 12 Qe2 Ngf6 13 0–0–0 0–0–0 14 Ne5 with pressure.

NIMZOWITSCH'S DEFENCE

This (**1 e4 Nc6**) is very rarely played. I'm giving it in detail only because readers might like to use it, when Black, as a surprise weapon. The recommended reply is 2 d4 d5 3 Nc3 de 4 d5 Nb8 5 Bf4 Nf6 6 Bc4 c6 7 Nge2 cd 8 N×d5, but many players after Black's 4 . . . Nb8 will begin to treat the position casually; and that can be a fatal mistake. Black has another way of handling the defence after 1 e4 Nc6 2 d4 by 2 . . . e5 3 de N×e5 4 f4 Ng6 (diag 248); Black threatens . . . Bc5 commanding the c5–g1 diagonal;

White should get there first by 5 Be3, when there could follow 5 . . . Bb4+ 6 c3 Ba5 with an unclear position—maybe Black is okay.

From this repertoire one goes on over the months building up a more detailed network acquired by personal experience and from the study of master games. If you are ambitious you will want to master the problems and intricacies of your chosen lines and hope thereby to control the direction of play.

But do not rely on opening knowledge to bring you more than partial success. Against real chessplayers it will not alone suffice.

If you are one of those who constantly varies your openings you will be entertained by a wide range of positions. But you must occasionally expect to be at the receiving end of unpleasant shocks and forced to work hard and consume a lot of time trying to survive.

Finally there is an argument for changing one's repertoire every year or two in order to combat staleness and routine if so affected.

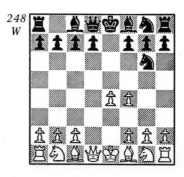

248
W

7 Great players, games and positions

The first international chess event on record was held at Madrid in 1574 on the occasion of the visit of the Calabrian (Italian), Giovanni Leonardo, who beat the two best Spanish players, Ruy Lopez and Ceron, in the presence of King Philip II.

Philidor

André Philidor (1726–1795), a French musical composer (23 operas), was the first great master of the chessboard whose talent we can measure in the only acceptable way by an examination of the records of his games. (See also comment on Philidor, p. 45). (See p. 91 for an explanation of descriptive notation).

Here is one of two blindfold simultaneous games played in London in 1783. White: **Count Brühl**, Black **Philidor**. 1 P–K4 P–K4 2 B–B4 P–QB3 3 Q–K2 P–Q3 4 P–QB3 P–KB4 5 P–Q3 N–B3 6 P×P B×P 7 P–Q4 P–K5 8 B–KN5 P–Q4 9 B–N3 B–Q3 10 N–Q2 N1–Q2 11 P–KR3 P–KR3 12 B–K3 Q–K2 13 P–KB4? (Imprisoning his own dark-squared bishop) 13 ... P–KR4! 14 P–B4 P–R3 15 P×P P×P 16 Q–B2 0–0 17 N–K2 P–QN4 18 0–0 N–N3 19 N–N3 P–N3 20 QR–B1 N–B5 21 N×B P×N 22 Q–N3+ Q–N2! 23 Q×Q+ K×Q 24 B×N NP×B 25 P–KN3 QR–N1 26 P–N3 B–R6 27 R–QB2 P×P 28 P×P (28 N×P was better) 28 ... R/B1–B1 29 R×R R×R 30 R–R1 B–N5 31 R×P R–B6 32 K–B2 R–Q6 33 R–R2 B×N 34 R×B R×NP 35 R–B2 P–R5! (diag 249) 36 R–B7+ K–N3 37 P×P N–R4 38 R–Q7 N×P! 39 B×N R–KB6+ 40 K–N2 R×B 41 R×P R–B6 42 R–Q8 R–Q6 43 P–Q5 P–B5 44 P–Q6 R–Q7+ 47 K–B1 K–B2! 46 P–R5 P–K6 47 P–R6 P–B6 White resigned. Black mates or queens first.

Sarratt, La Bourdonnais and Staunton

The first great British player was J. H. Sarratt, who won renown as a master of real attacking ability, a codifier of rules and a writer (Treatise—1808 and New Treatise—posthumously in 1821). The centre of world chess during the nineteenth-century veered between Paris and London, with North America coming into the picture in the 1880s and '90s. A famous series of matches between Louis Charles Mahé de la Bourdonnais (1795–1840) of France and Alexander MacDonnell (born Belfast, 1798–1835) at the Westminster Club in 1834 resulted in wins for the Frenchman 16–5 (with 4 draws) followed by 28–22 (9 draws). The prestige balance switched back to England when Howard Staunton (1810–74) met Pierre Charles Fournier de Saint-Amant (1800–72) at the Cercle d'Echecs, Paris in 1843 and was the victor by 11 wins, six losses and 4 drawn.

La Bourdonnais–MacDonnell, game 17; Queen's Gambit Accepted— 1 P–Q4 P–Q4 2 P–QB4 P×P 3 P–K3 P–K4! 4 B×P P×P 5 P×P N–KB3 6 N–QB3 B–K2 7 N–B3 0–0 8 B–K3 P–B3 9 P–KR3! (White, with a reasonable mobilisation of pieces, is justified in depriving Black of a good square for the bishop and knight.) 9 ... QN–Q2 10 B–N3 N–N3 11 0–0 N/B3–Q4 12 P–QR4 P–QR4 13 N–K5 B–K3 14 B–B2 P–KB4?! 15 Q–K2 P–B5 16 B–Q2 Q–K1 17 QR–K1 B–B2 18 Q–K4 P–KN3 19 B×P! N×B 20

249
W

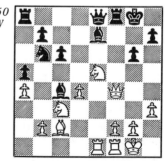

250
W

Q×N B–B5 (diag 250) 21 Q–R6! B×R 22 B×P! P×B 23 N×P N–B1
(*23 . . . B–B3!?*) 24 Q–R8+ K–B2 25 Q–R7+ K–B3 26 N–B4! B–Q6 27
R–K6+ K–N4 28 Q–R6+ K–B4 29 P–KN4 mate.

Anderssen

The first big international tournament was stages in London in 1851, the
year of the 'Great Exhibition of Art and Industry' at the Crystal Palace;
it was a knock-out event with 16 players; the German player Adolf Anderssen (1818–79) beat Staunton in the semi-final 4–1 and Marmeduke Wyvill
in the final by 4–2. Diagram 179 shows the position from which Anderssen
won the 'evergreen' game in 1852.

The 'immortal game' is how **Anderssen–Kieseritsky**, London 1851 is
designated—it went 1 e4 e5 2 f4 ef 3 Bc4 Qh4+ 4 Kf1 b5 5 B×b5 Nf6 6
Nf3 Qh6 7 d3 Nh5 8 Nh4 Qg5 9 Nf5 c6? (*9 . . . g6!*) 10 Rg1! cb 11 g4 Nf6
12 h4 Qg6 13 h5 Qg5 14 Qf3 Ng8 15 B×f4 Qf6 16 Nc3 Bc5 17 Nd5 Q×b2
(diag 251) 18 Bd6!!? (*18 Be3! Q×a1+ 19 Kg2 Q×g1+ 20 B×g1 leaves
Black no defence.*) 18 . . . B×g1 (*Better 18 . . . Q×a1+ 19 Ke2 Qb2!*)
19 e5!! Sacrificing two rooks in order to construct a mating net. 19 . . .
Q×a1+ 20 Ke2 (*Threat is 21 N×g7+ Kd8 22 Bc7 mate.*) 20 . . . Na6 21
N×g7+ Kd8 22 Qf6+! N×f6 23 Be7 mate.

Morphy

Paul Morphy (1837–84) is the first great American player. Phenomenon is
a better description. In the course of two years he rose to dominate the chess
world as a player, to add a new dimension to chess thinking and to retire
back to obscurity in New Orleans. Morphy won the first American congress
in 1857 and sailed to Europe intent on toppling Staunton from a throne
which the Englishman, no longer physically fit, did not want to occupy.
The American convincingly established his superiority; at the end of 1858
in Paris he beat Anderssen 7–2, 2 drawn. Staunton evaded a serious contest,
and, in doing so, added unknowingly to the onset of the persecution complex and melancholia that was to afflict Morphy in his later years.

Morphy–Löwenthal, match, London 1858: 1 P–K4 P–K4 2 N–KB3
N–QB3 3 B–N5 P–QR3 4 B–R4 N–B3 5 P–Q4 P×P 6 P–K5 N–K5 7 0–0

N–B4 8 B×N QP×B 9 N×P N–K3?! 10 N×N B×N 11 Q–K2 B–QB4
12 N–B3 Q–K2 13 N–K4 P–R3 14 B–K3! (*To control diagonal g1–a7 and
have possibility of f2–f4–f5*) 14 . . . B×B 15 Q×B B–B4? (*15 . . . 0–0!*)
16 N–N3 B×P? 17 P–B4 P–KN3 (diag 252) 18 P–K6! (*Threatening 19
Q–QB3 attacking bishop and rook. If now 18 . . . 0–0–0 19 Q–R7.*) 18 . . .
B–B4 19 N×B P×N 20 P×P+ K×P 21 Q–KR3 Q–B3 22 QR–K1
KR–K1 23 R–K5! K–N3 24 R/B1–K1 R×R 25 R×R R–Q1 26 Q–N3+

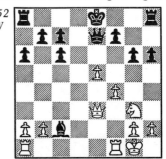

251
W

252
W

K–R2. Black has problems as his king has less shelter available. 27 P–KR3 R–Q2 28 Q–K3 P–N3 29 K–R2 P–B4 30 Q–K2 Q–N3 31 R–K6 Q–N2 32 Q–R5 R–Q4 (*If 32 . . . R–B2 33 R × RP+*) 33 P–QN3 P–N4 (*Or 33 . . . P–R4 34 P–QR4*) 34 R × QRP R–Q3 35 Q × BP+ Q–N3 36 Q × Q+ K × Q 37 R–R5 R–N3 38 P–KN4 P–B3 39 K–N3 P–R4 40 R–R7 P × P 41 P × P K–B3 42 P–B5 K–K4 43 R–K7+ K–Q3 44 P–B6 R–N1 45 P–N5 R–KB1 46 K–B4 P–B5 47 P × P P × P 48 K–B5 P–B6 49 R–K3 Black resigned. *If 49 . . . P–B7 50 R–Q3+ K–B2 51 R–QB3 followed by advancing the connected passed pawns.*

Steinitz

Wilhelm Steinitz, (1836–1900), from Bohemia, beat Anderssen in 1866 (8 wins, six losses, no draws!) and for the next 28 years can be regarded as the world's leading player. The match in 1886 between Steinitz and Johannes Hermann Zukertort (1842–88, who was born in Poland) is the first to be generally recognised as being for the world championship title. It was a fluctuating event. After five games in New York Zukertort led by four wins to one; Steinitz won four and drew one of the St. Louis phase to gain an overall lead 5½–4½; in the final phase at New Orleans Zukertort became exhausted and Steinitz won by 10–5, 5 draws.

One of the great games of the last century was **Steinitz's** win over **von Bardeleben** at Hastings in 1895. Steinitz had lost a match with Emmanuel Lasker for the world title the previous year.)

Steinitz was White: **1 e2–e4 e7–e5 2 Ng1–f3 Nb8–c6 3 Bf1–c4 Bf8–c5 4 c2–c3 Ng8–f6 5 d2–d4.** White is hoping to set up a pawn centre that will be both aggressive and cramping. **5 . . . e5 × d4 6 c3 × d4 Bc5–b4+ 7 Nb1–c3.** See p. 53 for more on these variations. **7 . . . d7–d5** Bardeleben wanted to exchange off one of the centre pawns. **8 e4 × d5 Nf6 × d5 9 0–0** Steinitz was aiming to mobilise the pieces quickly. If White were to play 9 B × d5 instead, Black could safely recapture 9 . . . Q × d5. **9 . . . Bc8–e6 10 Bc1–g5 Bb4–e7.**

Interest has re-awakened recently in this game through the attempts of some Russian analysts to explore in depth the possibilities of this famous brilliancy. Now Steinitz embarked on a series of exchanges of the pieces

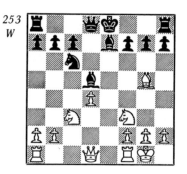

253
W

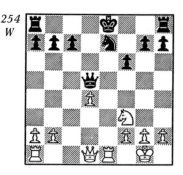

254
W

covering Black's king with a view to bringing the rooks to bear on it. **11 Bc4 × d5 Be6 × d5** (diag 253) **12 Nc3 × d5** The Russians have been looking at the similar idea 12 B × e7 N × e7 13 Re1, but it's not certain that it's an improvement. **12 . . . Qd8 × d5 13 Bg5 × e7 Nc6 × e7** There is some argument for Black to consider recapturing with the king, viz. 13 . . . K × e7!? 14 Re1+ Kf8 and if 15 Qe2, then 15 . . . g6 intending 16 . . . Kg7 and 17 . . . Rhe8. **14 Rfe1 f7–f6** (diag 254) Bardeleben would like to have followed this up with . . . Kf7 and then . . . Nd5. **15 Qd1–e2**

The Russians have also been investigating 15 Qa4+!? Kf7 16 Rac1; now best seems 16 . . . Qd6, planning to put the knight on d5, where it would act as an anchor for Black's position. They haven't come up with any line offering White clear prospects of an advantage, but all their efforts add perspective to the original game and show its true quality.

One line of theirs, that friends of mine have been examining in detail, runs 15 Qa4+ Kf7 16 Rac1 c6 17 R × e7+ K × e7 18 Qb4+ Kf7 19 Q × b7+ Kg6 when the Russian analysis went 20 R × c6—that threatens to win Black's queen by moving the rook again, this time with check—but after 20 . . . Rhc8, I couldn't find more than a draw through the knight perpetually checking, White having to watch his back rank. But, seeking an improvement we looked at 20 Ne5+! first, and only after 20 . . . f × e5 to play the rook move 21 R × c6+—this time more effectively as it is check—and with a further check available, White seems then to win.

255
W

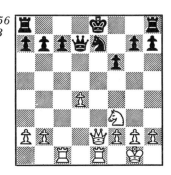

256
B

W. H. COZENS 1964

After 16 ... Kf7 the Russians have looked into 17 Ne5+ and 17 Ng5+, but Black survived those attempts also.

Now let's concentrate on the game. **17 d4–d5!** The d4 square is cleared to make room for the knight. **17 . . . c6×d5 18 Nf3–d4 Ke8–f7 19 Nd4–e6 Rh8–c8** This stops White's rook coming to c7. **20 Qe2–g4!** Steinitz thus threatened 21 Q×g7+ Ke8 22 Qf8 checkmate. **20 . . . g7–g6 21 Ne6–g5+** This check uncovers an attack of queen on to queen and **21 . . . Kf7–e8** was the only way to save the queen. Now the real attack begins! (diag 257) **22 Re1×e7+!** By this move, Steinitz shows a full appreciation of the tactical possibilities within the position. If 22 . . . Q×e7 with 23 R×c8+ R×c8 24 Q×c8+ White would have won a knight. For Black to recapture with the king would be even more disastrous—22 . . . K×e7 23 Re1+ Kd6 24 Qb4+ Kc7 25 Ne6+—and after the forced retreat 25 . . . Kb8 comes 26 Qf4+ Rc7 27 N×c7 Q×c7 28 Re8 mate.

Black saw this and played instead **22 . . . Ke8–f8**; the game proceeded **23 Re7–f7+** Not 23 Q×d7??—Black mates by 23 . . . R×c1. White must create the opportunity to take the queen with CHECK. **23 . . . Kf8–g8** If 23 . . . Q×f7 White again has 24 R×c8+. **24 Rf7–g7+ Kg8–h8** (diag 258) If the king had started to return by 24 . . . Kf8 White, by 25 N×h7+, would ensure the win of the black queen with check.

The last move played in the game was **25 R×h7+**; von Bardeleben had gone from the room and didn't return! When Black's time had run out, Steinitz was awarded the game and then demonstrated the forced finish

The actual game continued **15 . . . Qd5–d7** (diag 255); mate is stopped.

Another Russian probe here. They think that nothing seems to come from 16 d5, trying to force open the central files. But, paradoxically, 16 Rad1!, hiding the rook behind the pawn, has points. A sample line (*16 . . . Kf7 17 Qc4+ Nd5 18 Ne5+*), forces open lines after 18 . . . f×e5 19 d×e5 and threatens both e6+ and R×d5.

Again the game—**16 Ra1–c1** (diag 256) **16 . . . c7–c6** This attempt to solidify the position is probably the decisive error. It was pointed out in the tournament book published just after the 1895 congress, that Black could hold the position by 16 . . . Kf7! and, if 17 Q×e7+ Q×e7 18 R×e7+ K×e7 19 R×c7+, Black could defend his second rank by 19 . . . Kd6 followed by 20 . . . Rhc8 (threatening mate) and eventually 21 . . . Rc7.

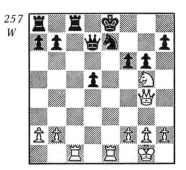

257
W

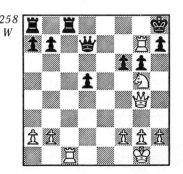

258
W

that he was intending—25 ... Kg8 26 Rg7+ Kh8 27 Qh4+ K×g7 28 Qh7 + Kf8 29 Qh8+ Ke7 30 Qg7+ Ke8 31 Qg8+ Ke7 32 Qf7+ Kd8 (*if 32 ... Kd6 33 Q×f6+ Qe6 34 Q×e6 MATE*) 33 Qf8+ Qe8 34 Nf7+ Kd7 35 Qd6 MATE. Who doesn't wish he could play as well as that!

Lasker

Dr Emanuel Lasker (born Germany 1868—died New York 1941), world champion from 1894 (he beat Steinitz 10–5, 4 draws) to 1921, was the fighter, philosopher and the intellectual at the chessboard. The first game of his title defence match in 1907 with USA's **Frank Marshall** (White) went 1 P–K4 P–K4 2 N–KB3 N–QB3 3 B–N5 N–B3 4 P–Q4 P×P 5 0–0 B–K2 6 P–K5 N–K5 7 N×P 0–0 8 N–B5 P–Q4 9 B×N P×B 10 N×B+ Q×N 11 R–K1 Q–R5 12 B–K3 P–B3 13 P–KB3 P×P 14 P×N P–Q5 15 P–KN3 (*If 15 B–Q2 B–N5 16 Q–B1 R–B7! 17 B–N5 R×NP+ 18 K×R B–R6+ should win.*) 15 ... Q–B3 16 B×P P×B 17 R–B1 Q×R+ 18 Q×Q R×Q+ 19 K×R (diag 259) It was surprising that Lasker had allowed the queens to be exchanged. At a casual glance the position looks even. But with a fine

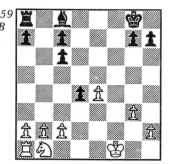

259
B

rook manoeuvre Lasker seizes the initiative. 19 ... R–N1! 20 P–N3 R–N4! (Here the rook has increased attacking possibilities. *If 21 N–Q2 R–KR4 22 K–N2 R–QB4 23 R–B1 B–R3 hoping for ... B–Q6.*) 22 P–B4 R–KR4 22 K–N1 (*On 22 P–KR4 P–N4!23 P×P R–R8+ sets up a permanent pin along the 8th rank.*) 22 ... P–B4 Making his third rank available for the rook. 23 N–Q2 K–B2! 24 R–KB1+ K–K2 25 P–QR3 R–R3 26 P–KR4 R–R3 27 R–QR1 B–N5 28 K–B2 K–K3 29 P–R4 K–K4 30 K–N2 R–KB3 31 R–K1 P–Q6 32 R–KB1 K–Q5 33 R×R P×R 34 K–B2 P–B3 35 P–QR5 P–QR3 36 N–B1 K×KP 37 K–K1 B–K7 38 N–Q2+ K–K6 39 N–N1 P–B4 40 N–Q2 P–R4 41 N–N1 K–B6 42 N–B3 K×P 43 N–R4 P–B5 44 N×P P–B6 45 N–K4+ K–B5 46 N–Q6 P–B4 47 P–N4 P×P 48 P–B5 P–N6 49 N–B4 K–N6 50 N–K3 P–N7 White resigned. A beautifully played and easy to understand ending!

Capablanca

José Raoul Capablanca (1888–1942), Cuban, world champion surprisingly for only six years (1921–27), played at the height of his career with an effortlessness that made all wonder that he could ever be beaten. When he took the title from Lasker in 1921 with four wins, no losses and ten draws there was only one fleeting instance in the whole of the match when Lasker might have gained a substantial advantage.

Capablanca–Janowski, played at St Petersburg 1914: 1 e4 e5 2 Nf3 Nc6 3 Bb5 a6 4 B×c6 dc 5 Nc3 Bc5 (*5 ... f6 is more usual and better.*) 6 d3 Bg4 7 Be3 B×e3? (*7 ... Qe7*) g fe Qe7 9 0–0 0–0–0? (*Janowski was probably unaware that he was running into any danger. He needed to castle on the other wing after 9 ... Nh6.*) 10 Qe1 Nh6 Capablanca had an almost unerring instinct as to which sector of the board to direct his energies as the next move shows. 11 Rb1!! (diag 260) White's centre is solid. A wing attack is appropriate; and Janowski can do nothing about this one. 11 ... f6 12 b4 Nf7 13 a4 B×f3 14 R×f3 b6? (*It would have been better to play 14 ... b5 and follow up with ... Kb7 and ... Ra8.*) 15 b5! cb 16 ab a5 17 Nd5 Qc5 18 c4! Ng5 19 Rf2! Ne6 20 Qc3 Rd7 21 Rd1! Kb7 22 d4 Qd6 23 Rc2 ed 24 ed Nf4 25 c5 N×d5 26 ed Q×d5 27 c6+ Kb8 28 cd Q×d7 29 d5 Re8 30 d6 cd 31 Qc6 Black resigned.

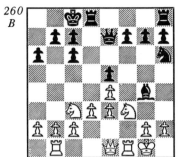

260
B

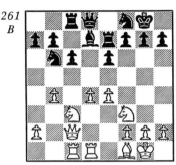

261
B

Capablanca Lasker, 11th game, 1921 match: 1 P–Q4 P–Q4 2 N–KB3 P–K3 3 P–QB4 N–KB3 4 B–N5 QN–Q2 5 P–K3 B–K2 6 N–B3 0–0 7 R–B1 R–K1 8 Q–B2 P–B3 9 B–Q3 P×P 10 B×BP N–Q4 11 B×B R×B? (*Better and usual is 11 . . . Q×B 12 0–0 N×N 13 Q×N P–K4*) 12 0–0 N–B1 (*12 . . . N×N 13 Q×N P–QN3 would be more vigorous.*) 13 KR–Q1 B–Q2 14 P–K4 N–N3?! 15 B–B1 R–B1 16 P–QN4 (diag 261) 16 . . . B–K1 17 Q–N3 R2–B2 18 P–QR4 N–N3 19 P–R5 N–Q2 20 P–K5 (*With a post at Q6 for the knight*) 20 . . . P–N3 21 N–K4 R–N1 22 Q–B3 (*22 Q–R3 would have been more exact. Black's knight now comes to its Q4 with a gain of tempo.*) 22 . . . N–B5 23 N–Q6 N–Q4 24 Q–R3 P–B3!? (*24 . . . Q–K2!?*) 25 N×B! Q×N 26 KP×P KNP×P 27 P–N5! R1–B1 28 NP×P R×P 29 R×R R×R 30 P×P P×P 31 R–K1 White's queen's side initiative has been exchanged for a weakened black king's position. 31 . . . Q–QB1 32 N–Q2 N–B1 33 N–K4 Q–Q1 34 P–R4! (*Against Black's plan of 34 . . . P–B4—followed by 35 . . . R–B6 and 36 . . . Q–N4—Capablanca had prepared 35 Q–KN3+! K–R1 36 Q–K5+ K–N1 37 B–N5 R–B2 38 N–N5 R–K2 39 B–B4 N–B2 40 P–R5! P–N4 41 B–N3 when Black cannot cope with both P–Q5 and N×KP.*) 34 . . . R–B2?! (*Capablanca suggested 34 . . . P–R3, preparing for . . . P–B4.*) 35 Q–QN3 R–KN2! 36 P–N3 R–R2 37 B–B4 (*Threat to take twice on Q5*) 37 . . . R–R4 38 N–B3 N×N 39 Q×N K–B2 40 Q–K3 Q–Q3 41 Q–K4 R–R5?! (*41 . . . R–R2*) 42 Q–N7+ K–N3 (*If 42 . . . Q–K2 43 Q–B6*) 43 Q–B8 Q–N5 44 R–QB1 Q–K2 45 B–Q3+ K–R3 46 R–B7 R–R8+ 47 K–N2 Q–Q3 48 Q×N+! Black resigned. Relentless machine-like chess with Lasker always under pressure.

Rubinstein

When Capablanca emerged after the San Sebastian tournament 1911 as a world class player, Lasker's other potential challenger was the Polish player, Akiba Rubinstein. In the 1907 tournament at Lodz, **Rubinstein**, as Black, won from the position in diagram 262 in most striking fashion. First came the startling 1 . . . R×c3!! allowing White to take the queen by 2 gh (*If 2 B×c3 B×e4+ 3 Q×e4 Q×h2 mate or 2 B×b7 R×g3 3 Rf3 R×f3 4 B×f3 Nf2+ 5 Kg1 Ne4+ 6 Kf1 Nd2+ 7 Kg2 N×f3 8 Q×f3 Rd2+ wins*) 2 . . . Rd2!! A further surprising deflection. After 3 Q×d2 B×e4+ 4 Qg2 Rh3! and, as mate cannot be put off for more than three moves, White (**Rotlewi**) resigned.

Rubinstein–Capablanca, played at San Sebastian 1911: 1 P–Q4 P–Q4 2 N–KB3 P–QB4 3 P–B4 P–K3 4 BP×P KP×P 5 N–B3 N–QB3 6 P–KN3 B–K3 (*Nowadays 6 . . . N–B3 7 B–N2 B–K2 8 0–0 0–0 is the accepted order.*) 7 B–N2 B–K2 8 0–0 R–B1 9 P×P B×P 10 N–KN5 N–B3 11 N×B P×N 12 B–R3 Q–K2 13 B–N5 0–0 14 B×N! Q×B (*If 14 . . . R×B 15 N×P P×N 16 B×R*) 15 N×P! (diag 263. *On the surface this is a very simple combination—if 15 . . . P×N 16 Q×P+ K–R1 17 B×R wins material; the desperado combination 15 . . . B×P+ 16 K–N2 Q–R3 17 N–B4 offers no relief. But it's when the side variations are calculated that its profoundness becomes apparent.*) 15 . . . Q–R3! (*As 16 N–B4 is met by 16 . . . R×N*) 16 K–N2 R/QB1–Q1! (*Has Rubinstein miscalculated?*) 17 Q–B1!! (*No! It slowly penetrates that this was one of the rare occasions*

262
B

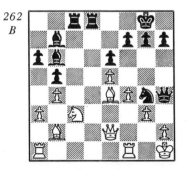

263
B

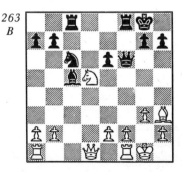

when someone had seen further than the great Cuban. *If 17 ... R×N 18 Q×Q P×Q 19 B×P+)* **17 ... P×N 18 Q×B Q–Q7** Rubinstein will need to play very well to cash his extra pawn in the face of the active black pieces. **19 Q–N5 N–Q5 20 Q–Q3 Q×Q 21 P×Q R/B1–K1 22 B–N4!** (*22 R/B1–K1 N–B7 23 R×R+ R×R 24 R–QB1 N–K8+ would give Black counterplay.*) **22 ... R–Q3! 23 R/B1–K1 R×R 24 R×R R–QN3 25 R–K5! R×P 26 R×P N–B3 27 B–K6+ K–B1 28 R–KB5+ K–K1 29 B–B7+ K–Q2 30 B–B4** (*This threatens to force the exchange of rooks by R–N5.*) **30 ... P–QR3 31 R–B7+ K–Q3 32 R×KNP P–N4 33 B–N8 P–QR4 34 R×P P–R5 35 P–KR4 P–N5 36 R–R6+ K–B4 37 R–R5+ K–N3** (*If 37 ... K–Q5 38 R–Q5+ leads to the win of the knight.*) **38 B–Q5?!** (*A tiny flaw in what otherwise seems a perfectly played game—38 B–B4 would have been better as White would then have the possibility of R–QN5+ in some variations.*) **38 ... P–N6?!** (*Rubinstein would have found the game much harder to win after 38 ... R×RP!! as Black can promote after 39 B×R P–N6; best 39 B–B4 R–QB7! 40 R–QN5+ K–B2 41 B–N8.*) **39 P×P! P–R6** (*If 39 ... P×P 40 R–R6*) **40 B×N! R×NP** (*On 40 ... P–R7 White would have 41 R–N5+ K–R3 42 R–N8 P–R8=Q 43 R–QR8+ skewering.*) **41 B–Q5 P–R7 42 R–R6+!** Black resigned. If the king is played to the QR file White has R–R8, while 42 ... K–N4 also enables White to reach the QR file after 43 B–B4+. Rubinstein was very proud of this great win.

Alekhine

If Capablanca's contribution to chess was his effortless virtuosity which showed that men may master chess and become unbeatable, and unfortunately, that chess may have become played out, Alekhine's contribution was to demonstrate that where the will existed there was still limitless scope for attack, for complications and for new ideas. The advent of the Soviet School in the thirties served to confirm this viewpoint, and the successes of Bobby Fischer to strengthen this further.

Alexander Alekhine (1892–1946) surprised the chess world when he beat Capablanca in 1927 after a titanic struggle by 6–3, with 25 draws. Capablanca had had his greatest tournament success at New York a few months earlier. Alekhine, an exiled Russian, living in Paris, had achieved

the impossible after a super-human exercise in discipline and restraint; he won in his opponent's style.

Examples from Alekhine can be found on pp. 14, 39 and 72. His greatest tournament triumph was at San Remo in 1930 where his score of 13 wins and 2 unwilling draws out-distanced the rest of the field by 3½ points. **Alekhine**'s most satisfying win there must have been the one over his great rival Aron **Nimzowitsch**. Alekhine is White—1 e4 e6 2 d4 d5 3 Nc3 Bb4 4 e5 c5 5 Bd2 Ne7 6 Nb5 B×d2+ 7 Q×d2 0–0 8 c3 b6 (*Better 8 ... Nf5 followed by ... Bd7*) 9 f4 Ba6 10 Nf3 Qd7 11 a4 Nbc6 12 b4! cb 13 cb Bb7 14 Nd6 f5? (*14 ... a5, to aim for more elbow room, is better.*) 15 a5! Nc8 16 N×b7 Q×b7 17 a6 Qf7 18 Bb5 N8e7 19 0–0 h6 20 Rfc1 Rec8 21 Rc2 Qe8 22 Rac1 (*22 Ra3! followed by Rac3 and Qc1 is more exact.*) 22 ... Rab8 23 Qe3 Rc7 24 Rc3! Qd7 25 R1c2 Kf8 26 Qc1 Rbc8 27 Ba4! Black is running out of playable moves. 27 ... b5 28 B×b5 Ke8 29 Ba4 Kd8 30 h4 (diag 264) Black resigned. After 30 ... Qe8 31 b5 Black's position collapses.

264
B

Euwe

Holland's Dr Machgielis Euwe (b. 1901) added another shock result when he took Alekhine's world title away from him in 1935 for two years. But it is for his writings, expounding the strategic ideas of the chessboard, that Euwe is best appreciated. **Geller–Euwe, Zürich 1953**, is a fine win, viz. **1 P–Q4 N–KB3 2 P–QB4 P–K3 3 N–QB3 B–N5 4 P–K3 P–B4 5 P–QR3 B×N+ 6 P×B P–QN3 7 B–Q3 B–N2 8 P–B3 N–B3 9 N–K2 0–0 10 0–0 N–QR4 11 P–K4 N–K1** In order to contain a white pawn centre after 12 B–K3 P–Q3 13 N–N3 Q–Q2 14 P–B4 with 14 . . . P–KB4. **12 N–N3! P×P 13 P×P R–B1** With pressure on White's QBP. If 13 Q–R4 B–R3 or 13 Q–K2 N–N6 or 13 Q–B2 N×P 14 B×N P–Q4 **14 P–B4 N×P 15 P–B5** With the threat 16 P–B6 N×P 17 B–N5 breaking up the pawns round the black king. **15 . . . P–B3 16 R–B4!** P–QN4 Another plan is 16 . . . P–K4 17 R–R4 P×P 18 Q–R5 N–K4! **17 R–R4 Q–N3 18 P–K5!** Protecting his QP and preparing to open the diagonal of his bishop at Q3. **18 . . . N×KP 19 P×P N×B 20 Q×N Q×KP! 21 Q×RP+ K–B2 22 B–R6** (diag 265) **22 . . . R–KR1! 23 Q×R R–B7** The other rook was sacrificed in order to enable Black thus to seize the initiative. **24 R–QB1?** 24 P–Q5 would have been somewhat better. **24 . . . R×P+ 25 K–B1 Q–N6!** With two mate threats from . . . Q–Q6+ or . . . Q–KB6+ **26 K–K1 Q–KB6** White resigned.

265
B

Botvinnik and the Soviet School

The greatest of the Soviet world champions is undoubtedly Mikhail Botvinnik. Following his example there emerged in the USSR a whole group of world championship class players who were to dominate the international scene from the 1940s till Fischer broke through at Reykjavik in 1972. These great masters were Vasily Smyslov (b. 1921, champion 1957–1958), David Bronstein (b. 1924, tied match 1951). Mikhail Tal (b. 1936, champion 1960–61), Tigran Petrosian (b. 1929, champion 1963–69) and Boris Spassky (b. 1937, champion 1969–72).

Botvinnik (b. 1911) clearly won the special world championship tournament organised in 1948, two years after Alekhine's death. But his supremacy was beginning to show in the great AVRO tournament in 1938 and was confirmed by the six player Soviet championship event of 1941. Botvinnik's hold on the world title was never strong; Bronstein and Smyslov drew 24 game matches with him in 1951 and 1954; Smyslov and Tal respectively beat him in 1957 and 1960, but lost return matches in the following year. Here is a Botvinnik game:

Botvinnik–Capablanca, AVRO 1938; **1 d4 Nf6 2 c4 e6 3 Nc3 Bb4 4 e3 d5 5 a3 B×c3+ 6 bc c5 7 cd ed 8 Bd3 0–0 9 Ne2 b6 10 0–0 Ba6 11 B×a6 N×a6 12 Bb2?!** 12 Qd3 is better; Black would try to meet this with 12 . . . Qc8. **12 . . . Qd7! 13 a4 Rfe8?** 13 . . . cd 14 cd Rfc8 would have been stronger. **14 Qd3 c4** Capablanca decides on the manoeuvre Na6–b8–c6–a5–b3 making White's pawn a4 a target. The balance of the game hinges on what play White can create elsewhere. **15 Qc2 Nb8 16 Rae1 Nc6** 16 . . . Nh5, preparing to play 17 . . . f5 and hold back or reduce the effect of White's king-side advance, has been suggested. **17 Ng3 Na5** If 17 . . . Ne4 18 Nh1! intending to return after 19 f3 **18 f3 Nb3 19 e4 Q×a4 20 e5 Nd7** Now threatening 21 . . . N6–B4 **21 Qf2 g6 22 f4 f5 23 exf6 N×f6 24 f5 R×e1 25 R×e1 Re8 26 Re6! R×e6 27 fe Kg7 28 Qf4!** Intending 29 Nf5+! gf 30 Qg5+ **28 . . . Qe8 29 Qe5 Qe7** Or 29 . . . Na5 30 Bc1! threatening 31 Qc7+ followed by Bh6 or 31 Bh6+. (diag 266) **30 Ba3!!** Botvinnik has derived his greatest pleasure from the making of this move. **30 . . . Q×a3** If 30 . . . Qe8 31 Qc7+ Kg8 32 Be7 Ng4 33 Qd7 wins **31 Nh5+! gh 32 Qg5+ Kf8 33 Q×f6+ Kg8 34 e7 Qc1+ 35 Kf2 Qc2+ 36 Kg3 Qd3+ 37**

Kh4 Qe4+ 38 K×h5 Qe2+ 39 Kh4 Qe4+ 40 g4 Qe1+ 41 Kh5 Black resigned.

Now follows a selection of games played by other leading members of the Soviet school:

Smyslov–Botvinnik, 9th game, match 1954: 1 e4 e6 2 d4 d5 3 Nc3 Bb4 4 e5 c5 5 a3 Ba5!? (*More usual is 5 . . . B×c3+ 6 bc Ne7.*) 6 b4! cd! 7 Qg4 Ne7 8 ba dc 9 Q×g7 Rg8 10 Q×h7 Nd7 11 Nf3 Nf8 (*11 . . . Qc7!?*) 12 Qd3 Q×a5 13 h4 Bd7 14 Bg5 Rc8 15 Nd4! (*Smyslov intends to meet 15 . . . Rc4 with 16 Qe3 Ra4 17 Rb1 R×a3 18 Nb5! with multi-threats.*) 15 . . . Nf5 16 Rb1! (*This parries 16 . . . N×d4 17 Q×d4 Bb5.*) 16 . . . Rc4 17 N×f5 ef 18 R×b7 Re4+?! (diag 267) 19 Q×e4! de 20 Rb8+ Bc8 21 Bb5+ Q×b5

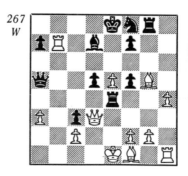

267
W

268
B

266
W

22 R×b5 Ne6 23 Bf6 R×g2 24 h5 Ba6 25 h6 Black resigned.

Pachman–Bronstein, Prague–Moscow 1946: 1 d4 Nf6 2 c4 d6 3 Nc3 e5 4 Nf3 Nbd7 5 g3 g6 6 Bg2 Bg7 7 0–0 0–0 8 b3 Re8 9 e4 ed 10 N×d4 Nc5 11 Re1 a5 12 Bb2 a4 13 Rac1 (*If 13 b4 a3!*) 13 . . . c6 14 Ba1 ab 15 ab Qb6 16 h3 Nfd7 (*Intending . . . Ndf8–e6 with increased pressure against b3*) 17 Rb1 Nf8 18 Kh2 (*Preparing f2–f4*) 18 . . . h5 19 Re2 (*If 19 f4 h4 20 g4 Nfe6*) 19 . . . h4 20 Rd2 (diag 268) 20 . . . R×a1!! (*Initiating a fantastic combination involving complex operations over the whole board.*) 21 R×a1 B×d4 22 R×d4 N×b3 23 R×d6 Q×f2!! (*Bronstein advanced the pawn to h4 on move 19 in order now to answer 24 Q×b3 with 24 . . . hg+ 25 Kh1 B×h3! 26 Rg1 B×g2+ 27 R×g2 Qf1+ 28 Rg1 Qh3 mate.*) 24 Ra2 Q×g3+ 25 Kh1 Q×c3 26 Ra3 (*If 26 Rd3 Qc1!*) 26 . . . B×h3 27 R×b3

B×g2+ 28 K×g2 Q×c4 29 Rd4 Qe6 30 R×b7 Ra8 31 Qe2 h3+ White resigned. This game helped considerably to popularise the defence used, the King's Indian.

Tal's play as a boy is depicted on p. 42. Here is **Tal–Suetin**, Tbilisi 1969–70: 1 e4 c5 2 Nf3 e6 3 d4 cd 4 N×d4 a6 5 Bd3 Ne7 (*5 . . . Nc6!*) 6 Nc3 Nbc6 7 Nb3 Ng6 8 0–0 b5 9 Be3 d6 10 f4 Be7 11 Qh5! (*If now Black goes 11 . . . 0–0 White has Rf1–f3–h3.*) 11 . . . Bf6 12 Rad1! B×c3?! (*Preferable is 12 . . . Qc7.*) 13 bc Qc7 14 Rd2 Ne7 (*Suetin hopes that his own position is safe and sound and that he can exploit the weakness of White's double c-pawns. Tal looks for a point of entry in Suetin's position.*) 15 Nd4! Bd7 16 f5! ef 17 ef Ne5 18 Ne6! B×e6 19 fe g6 (diag 269. *On hindsight 19 . . . 0–0–0 would have been safer.*) 20 Q×e5!! de 21 ef+ Black resigned. 21 . . . Kf8 would allow 22 Bh6 mate while after 21 . . . Kd7 22 Bf5++ Kc6 23 Be4+ would be murder.

Petrosian–Portisch, 13th game, match 1974: 1 Nf3 d5 2 d4 e6 3 c4 Nf6 4 Bg5 Be7 5 Nc3 0–0 6 Rc1 h6 7 Bh4 b6 8 cd N×d5 9 N×d5 ed 10 B×e7 Q×e7 11 g3 Ba6 (*Uhlmann–Veresov, East Germany–Byelorussia*

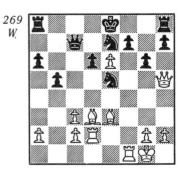

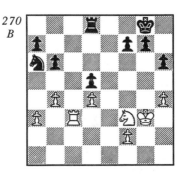

1971, went 11 . . . Re8 12 Bg2 Ba6 13 Ne5 Nd7 14 R×c7 Rac8!?) 12 e3 c5 13 B×a6 N×a6 14 0–0 Nc7 (*If 14 . . . c4 Portisch intended 15 b3.*) 15 b3 Rac8 16 Re1 Rfd8 17 h4 (*Against Black's manoeuvre Nc7–e6–g5*) 17 . . . Ne6 (*Possibility 17 . . . Ne8 to be followed by . . . Nf6 is better.*) 18 Qd3 Qf6 19 Kg2 cd 20 ed (*White could also retain some advantage by 20 R×c8 R×c8 21 ed to be followed by Re5 or Qa6.*) 20 . . . R×c1 21 R×c1 Qf4!? (*The queen is en route to either g4 or e4.*) 22 gf!! (*A remarkable approach to the position. In return for the pawn sacrificed White's pieces become active and the black knight is relegated to a series of out-of-the-way squares.*) 22 . . . N×f4+ 23 Kg3 N×d3 24 Rc3 Nb4 (*The improbable 24 . . . Nb2! 25 Rc2 Nd3 is a possibility.*) 25 a3 Na6 26 b4 (diag 270. *According to Petrosian Black could now try to hold his position with 26 . . . Rd7.*) 26 . . . Nb8 27 Rc7 a5 (*If 27 . . . a6 28 Ne5 f6 29 Ng6 leaves Black hard pressed.*) 28 b5! Nd7 29 Kf4 (*All the white pieces have potentially active roles.*) 29 . . . h5 (*Or 29 . . . Nf8 30 Rb7 Rd6 31 Ne5 Ng6 32 N×g6 fg 33 Ke5*) 30 Ne5 Nf8 31 Rb7 f6 32 Nc6 Ng6+ 33 Kg3 Rd6! 34 R×b6 Re6 35 Rb8+ Nf8 (*If 35 . . . Kh2 38 Rd8*) 36 Ra8 Re1 37 Nd8 (*37 b6 Rb1 38 Nb4 also wins.*) 37 . . . Kh7 38 b6 Rb1 39 b7 Nd7 40 R×a5 Black resigned.

For the Spassky–Rashkovsky game, with Spassky playing in his best style, turn to p. 43.

Paul Keres (Estonia, now USSR), Efim Geller (USSR) and Samuel Reshevsky (USA) were another three great rivals for Botvinnik. Here is a Keres' game.

Keres–Panno, Gothenburg 1955: **1 P–K4 P–QB4 2 N–KB3 P–Q3 3 P–Q4 P×P 4 N×P N–KB3 5 N–QB3 P–QR3 6 B–KN5 P–K3 7 P–B4 Q–N3 8 Q–Q2!** At the time of this game an original idea. With it Spassky scored one of his two actual wins over Fischer at Reykjavik. **8 . . . N–B3** Fischer played 8 . . . Q×NP. **9 0–0–0 Q×N 10 Q×Q N×Q 11 R×N N–Q2** If 11 . . . B–K2 12 B–K2 followed by KR–Q1 would give White a strong positional grip. **12 B–K2 P–R3 13 B–R4 P–KN4 14 P×P N–K4** On 14 . . . B–K2 White plays 15 B–N3. **15 N–R4! B–K2** White, after 15 . . . P–N4 16 N–N6 R–QN1 17 N×B R×N, can undermine Black's queen-side with 18 P–R4. **16 N–N6 R–QN1 17 B–N3 P×P 18 R/R1–Q1** (diag 271) White threatens 19 B×N P×B 20 R–B4. **18 . . . P–B3 19 P–B4 0–0** If 19 . . . B–Q2 20 P–B5 **20 R4–Q2 P–B4** Not wanting to remain passive. **21 P–B5 P–B5 22 P×P B×P 23 R×B P×B 24 P×P R–B2?!** *With 24 . . . N–B2! Black would show more fight.* **25 K–N1 R–B2 26 R–Q8+ K–N2 27 R–QB1! N–B3 28 P–K5 K–N3 29 B–Q3+ K–B2** *Or 29 . . . K–R4 30 R–R8+ K–N5 31 R–R3, threatening 32 R–B4 mate* **30 R–R8 K–K2 31 B–N6** Black resigned.

Fischer

Robert J. Fischer (USA, b. 9 March 1943) by beating Boris Spassky in 1972, became the first non-Soviet player to win the title since 1948. There follows three of his games:

Robert Byrne–Fischer, USA Championship Dec. 1963: **1 P–Q4 N–KB3**

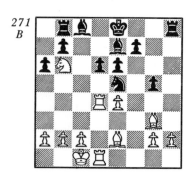

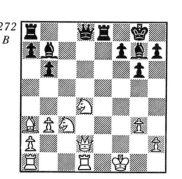

2 P–QB4 P–KN3 3 P–KN3 P–B3 4 B–N2 P–Q4 5 P×P P×P 6 N–QB3 B–N2 7 P–K3 0–0 8 KN–K2 N–B3 9 0–0 P–N3 10 P–N3 B–QR3 11 B–QR3 R–K1! **12 Q–Q2 P–K4! 13 P×P! N×P 14 KR–Q1** As analysis after the game showed this was the wrong rook. On 14 QR–Q1 Fischer suggested 14 . . . Q–B1 with about even opportunities. **14 . . . N–Q6! 15 Q–B2 N×P!! 16 K×N N–N5+ 17 K–N1 N×KP 18 Q–Q2 N×B!! 19 K×N P–Q5 20 N×P B–N2+ 21 K–B1** (diag 271) If 21 K–B2 Black can play for mate by 21 . . . Q–Q2 22 QR–B1 Q–R6 23 N–B3 B–KR3 24 Q–Q3 B–K6+. On 21 K–N1 Black has 21 . . . B×N+ 22 Q×B R–K8+! 23 K–B2 Q×Q 24 R×Q R×R. **21 . . . Q–Q2!!** and while the spectators in a side room were debating how Byrne would win, the news reached them that Byrne had resigned! He saw that if 22 Q–KB2 Q–R6+ 23 K–N1 the deflecting 23 . . . R–K8+ (and he was sure that Fischer would see it) 24 R×R B×N would force mate.

Tringov–Fischer, Havana 1965, with Fischer playing by Telex from New York: 1 e4 c5 2 Nf3 d6 3 d4 cd 4 N×d4 Nf6 5 Nc3 a6 6 Bg5 e6 7 f4 Qb6 8 Qd2 Q×b2 9 Rb1 Qa3 10 e5 de 11 fe Nfd7 12 Bc4 Bb4 13 Rb3 Qa5 14 0–0 0–0 15 N×e6!? fe 16 B×e6+ Kh8 17 R×f8+ B×f8 18 Qf4 (diag 273) 18 . . . Nc6! 19 Qf7 Qc5+ 20 Kh1 Nf6! 21 B×c8 (*If 21 ef B×e6 22 fg+ B×g7 23 Q×e6 Q×g5 or 21 B×f6 B×e6 22 Q×e6 gf 23 Q×f6+ Bg7 and Black would win in both cases.*) 21 . . . N×e5 22 Qe6 N5g4 and White resigned. This is typical of the complicated lines that Fischer, when Black, is willing to play and which he backs with painstaking study at home beforehand.

Fischer–Petrosian, 7th game, match 1971: **1 e4 c5 2 Nf3 e6 3 d4 cd 4 N×d4 a6 5 Bd3 Nc6 6 N×c6 bc 7 0–0 d5 8 c4 Nf6 9 cd cd 10 ed ed 11 Nc3 Be7 12 Qa4+!** (diag 274) Fischer, in his games, shows a marked trait to disrupt the even flow of an opponent's mobilisation. This intends, after 12 . . . Bd7 13 Qc2! 0–0 to put Black's pawns under pressure with 14 Bg5. **12 . . . Qd7!? 13 Re1!** This is much superior to winning the exchange—bishop for rook—by 13 Bb5. **13 . . . Q×a4 14 N×a4 Be6 15 Be3 0–0 16 Bc5!** In order to remove Black's potentially most active bishop. **16 . . . Rfe8** Livelier is 16 . . . B×c5 17 N×c5 Rfb8! **17 B×e7 R×e7 18 b4!** This keeps Black's a-pawn fixed for target practice. **18 . . . Kf8 19 Nc5**

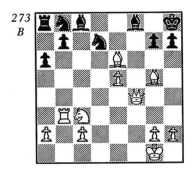

273
B

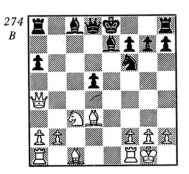

274
B

Bc8 20 f3 Rea7 21 Re5 Bd7! 22 N×d7+! R×d7 23 Rc1 24 Rc6 is the threat. 23 ... Rd6 24 Rc7 Nd7 25 Re2 Black is tied up; if his knight moves White has R2e7. 25 ... g6 26 Kf2 h5 27 f4 h4? 28 Kf3 f5 29 Ke3 d4+ 30 Kd2 Nb6 31 R2e7 Nd5 32 Rf7+ Ke8 33 Rb7 N×b4 34 Bc4 Black resigned. The threat is 35 Rh7 Rf6 36 Rh8+ Rf8 37 Bf7+ Kd8 38 R×f8 mate. The clarity of Fischer's positional play as White is in contrast to his approach when Black in the Tringov game.

1970-72 World Championship Series

Fischer won the world championship in 1972 after contesting a competition in three different phases. He was nominated in 1970 as one of the three USA qualifiers (or nominees) to the 1970 Interzonal Tournament.

1970 INTERZONAL

The 1970 Interzonal, under the auspices of the World Chess Federation (FIDE), was held at Palma de Mallorca and lasted for five weeks during which 24 qualifying grandmasters and masters, from different zones of the world, played one game against each other. The top six were to qualify for the 1971 Candidates phase. Bobby Fischer was first, scoring 15 wins 1 loss and 7 draws, 3½ points (1 point for win, ½ for draw), clear of the next players Bent Larsen (Denmark), Efim Geller (USSR) and Robert Hübner (West Germany) who were ahead of the two further qualifiers, Mark Taimanov (USSR) and Wolfgang Uhlmann (East Germany).

1971 CANDIDATES

The six qualifiers from the Interzonal joined Tigran Petrosian (USSR, losing world champion, 1969) and Victor Korchnoi (USSR, runner-up 1968 Candidates) to contest a series of knock-out matches.

In the quarter-finals: Fischer beat Taimanov in Vancouver 6–0! Petrosian beat Hübner (retired) in Seville 4–3; Larsen beat Uhlmann in Las Palmas 5½–3½; Korchnoi beat Geller in Sochi 5½–2½.

Semi-finals: Fischer beat Larsen in Denver 6–0! Petrosian beat Korchnoi in Moscow 5½–4½.

Final: Fischer beat Petrosian in Buenos Aires 6½–2½.

1972 WORLD CHAMPIONSHIP MATCH

Fischer beat Boris Spassky (USSR) at Reykjavik, in the most publicised chess match ever, by 7 wins, 2 losses plus 1 forfeited, and 11 draws.

Ten zonal tournaments to determine the qualifiers for the 1973 Interzonal Tournaments were held during 1972.

Two Interzonal Tournaments, with 18 qualifiers and seeded players in each, were held during 1973. In the Leningrad Interzonal the three to go forward to the 1974 Candidates Matches were Anatoly Karpov and Victor

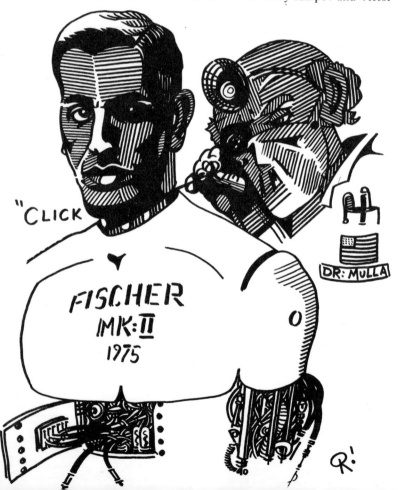

Korchnoi (both USSR) and Robert Byrne (USA). The qualifiers from the Petropolis (Brazil) Interzonal were Henrique Mecking (Brazil), Lev Polugayevsky (USSR) and Lajos Portisch (Hungary).

1974 CANDIDATES

In the quarter-finals: Spassky beat Byrne in Puerto Rica 3–0, 3 draws; Karpov beat Polugayevsky in Moscow 3–0, 5 draws; Petrosian beat Portisch in Palma de Mallorca 3–2, 8 draws; Korchnoi beat Mecking in Augusta 3–1, 9 draws.

Semi-finals: Karpov beat Spassky in Leningrad 4–1, 6 draws; Korchnoi beat Petrosian in Odessa 3–1, 1 draw, retired ill.

Final: Karpov is to play Korchnoi for the first to win five games.

WORLD CHAMPIONSHIP MATCH 1975

The winner of the 1974 Candidates matches is scheduled to play a match with the holder, Robert J. Fischer, for the world championship title starting on 1 June, 1975. The first to win six games will be the winner.

Whether Anatoly Karpov becomes Fischer's challenger from the current series or not, many regard this young man (b. 23 May, 1951) as a future world champion.

Adams

Edward Adams is known in chess circles only for his play in one game. Played in New Orleans in 1920, that game has become one of the classics of chess! Adams had White against the Mexican master, Carlos Torre, then sixteen years old. The opening is colourless, but the end of the game is distinguished by the perfect exploitation of Black's back rank weakness.

The game began **1 e2–e4 e7–e5 2 Ng1–f3 d7–d6** This is known as Philidor's Defence. It's not particularly popular, no doubt due to the self-imposed limiting of the bishop at f8. **3 d2–d4** This opens up more lines for the white pieces and threatens to win a pawn by 4 d4 × e5 d6 × e5 5 Q × d8+ K × d8 6 N × e5! **3 . . . e5 × d4** This is unusual, but it has been played in recent years by the famous Danish grandmaster, Bent Larsen. **4 Qd1 × d4** Taking with the knight is equally playable; in reply Black would play 4 . . . g6, intending to 'fianchetto' his f8 bishop at g7. **4 . . . Nb8–c6** Attacking White's queen; the reply, **5 Bf1–b5**, pins the knight to the diagonal of

the black king. **5 . . . Bc8–d7** Unpinning and renewing the attack on White's queen. **6 Bb5×c6 Bd7×c6** The white queen has an untroubled, dominant position (diag 275). **7 Nb1–c3 Ng8–f6** Both players develop their pieces. **8 0–0** Maybe better is 8 Bg5, followed by 0–0–0 and then, either Rhe1 or some advance of the f, g and h pawns if Black should castle on that wing. **8 . . . Bf8–e7 9 Nc3–d5** This post is sometimes ideal for a knight, but here it is quickly swapped off without White gaining any advantage; however, Black can't afford 9 . . . N×d5 as 10 ed hits Black's bishop and leaves his position in a tangle, e.g. on 10 . . . Bf6 White can win a piece by 11 Qe4+.

9 . . . Bc6×d5 If this exchange is delayed—say Black castles instead—White supports the knight with his c-pawn and gains more space for manoeuvring. **10 e4×d5 0–0 11 Bc1–g5** (diag 276) **11 . . . c7–c6** 11 . . . N×d5 is answered simply by 12 Q×d5, adding to the protection of the bishop. But Black could prepare such a combination; it would work after 11 . . . h6! 12 Bh4 N×d5 13 Q×d5 B×h4 14 N×h4 Q×h4 15 Qb7 Qc4 when Black has no difficulties. The additional advantage of the pawn move 11 . . . h6 is that Black's king has an escape square from the back row, the lack of which he will regret.

12 c2–c4 c6×d5 13 c4×d5 Rf8–e8 14 Rf1–e1 a7–a5 15 Re1–e2 White is starting to double the rooks. **15 . . . Ra8–c8** Torre, not fully alert to the critical nature of his problems along the e-file, continues formal development. Instead 15 . . . Nd7! would have been better; then if White doubles by 16 Rae1 Black can go 16 . . . f6 followed by 17 . . . Ne5.

After the moved played, White produces a series of dazzling moves, as

275
W

276
B

well-conceived and relevant as the finest play of the greatest masters. **16 Ra1–e1.** With this doubling of the rooks, White threatens 17 B×f6; then recapture by the bishop would cost Black his queen for a rook, viz. 17 . . . B×f6 18 R×e8+ Q×e8 19 R×e8+; the pawn recapture weakens Black's king's position. **16 . . . Qd8–d7 17 Bg5×f6** (diag. 277) **17 . . . Be7×f6**

17 . . . g7×f6 would have been comparatively better. It sets a subtle trap: if then White plays 18 R×e7 hoping for 18 . . . R×e7 19 R×e7 Q×e7 20 Qg4 forking king and rook, Black would play 18 . . . Q×e7!! as White's own back row would be inadequately guarded—19 R×e7 Rc1+.

In the game again, with White to move. At the moment Black needs both his rook at c8 and queen at d7 to protect his rook at e8 against capture and mate. Therefore both guardians have limited scope in other directions.

18 Qd4–g4!! Black's queen is attacked and it must stay on the a4–d7 diagonal to protect the e8 rook. **18 . . . Qd7–b5** A curious situation: Black threatens 19 . . . Q×e2 and if White recaptures by 20 R×e2 Black mates 20 . . . Rc1—21 Re1 R×e1+ 22 N×e1 R×e1. **19 Qg4–c4!!** This shuts out Black's idea, and bears on both of the e8-rook's defenders. **19 . . . Qb5–d7 20 Qc4–c7!** It's the same story—White's queen cannot be taken, and Black's queen must be found a safe square along the e8–a4 diagonal. **20 . . . Qd7–b5** If 20 . . . Qa4 White wins by 21 Re4! as this rook move involves the desperado combination 21 . . . Rf8 22 Q×c8 Q×e4 23 Q×f8+ winning a rook. White also must be careful; the 'brilliant' 21 Q×b7?! would have come to grief against Black's 21 . . . Q×e2 22 Q×c8 Q×e1+.

The game continued **21 a2–a4** (diag 278) **21 . . . Qb5×a4** (Two other variations must be calculated:—if 21 . . . R×e2 then 22 Q×c8+ or 21 . . . Q×e2 when 22 R×e2 leaves Black helpless.)

Play went **22 Re2–e4 Qa4–b5.** Black could have tried two other ideas:
1) 22 . . . h6 23 Q×c8 Q×e4 24 Q×e8+ which loses him a rook, and
2) 22 . . . Kf8 23 Q×d6+ Be7 24 R×e7 with White winning at least a bishop. Black has no defence.

The game finished with **23 Qc7×b7.** This is now possible with white's rook on e4 instead of at e2. Black cannot save both his king and queen, and so he resigned the game. Wonderful play by Edward Adams!

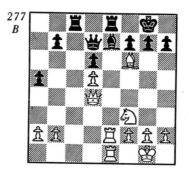
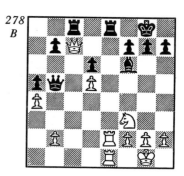

277 B

278 B

Computer Game

The next game is one played between two electronic computers! But first a little background on computer chess seems in order.

People have always been fascinated by the idea of a machine that could play chess, and it is not really surprising that in 1770 a young Austrian engineer named Wolfgang Kempelen constructed an ingenious machine that won nearly every game it ever played. This machine, 'The Turk', defeated Napoleon in 1809 and subsequent imitations also performed famous feats and made money for their inventors. These 'machines' were all frauds, of course,—inside each, a small but strong human chess master was cunningly concealed!

True computer chess dates from 1950, not long after the first electonic 'brains' were invented. An American, Claude Shannon, developed in 1950 the first chess-playing programme which, though very humble, could defeat untutored human players. Shannon's programme involved translating the values (material and positional) of the chess-board into numbers, and on this basis a lot of work has been done in the last 25 years—especially in the USA, and in the USSR, where ex-world champion Mikhail Botvinnik, has been a moving force.

Botvinnik's claim that there will be, before long, computer masters and grandmasters, is not, however, taken seriously by many informed people. The difficulty seems to lie as much with the human programmers, who cannot express mathematically the intuitive processes of a master, as with the technical capacities of the machines. There are still many bugs to be ironed out of existing programmes. For instance, in this position (diag 279) from the competition of the 1973 conference of the Association for Computing Machinery at Atlanta, the 'Coko IV' programme, being played against programme 'Tech', and undoubtedly losing, shocked everyone with the suicidal **44 Qe7+**.

David Levy, the Scottish international master, is likely to win his £1000 bet that no computer programme will be able to beat him by August 1978! However, advances in computer technology may one day allow machines to work in methods even more analogous to the human brain—which is not restricted to numerical calculation.

The following game, played between two of the ablest programmes in 1966–67 (just before Levy's bet was taken), will give a fair indication of computer chess capabilities. White was the Moscow ITEP programme and Black was John McCarthy's Stamford University system. The game went: **1 e4 e5 2 Nf3 Nc6 3 Nc3 Bc5?! 4 N×e5 N×e5? 5 d4 Bd6 6 d4×e5 B×e5 7 f4 B×c3+ 8 b2×c3 Nf6? 9 e5 Ne4 (see diag 280) 10 Qd3?!**

A stronger move was 10 Qd5!, but the Russian computer, calculating only 2½ moves deep, could not help rejecting this possibility.

10...Nc5 11 Qd5 Ne6? 12 f5 Ng5 13 h4 f6 14 h4×g5 f6×g5 15 R×h7 Rf8 16 R×g7 c6 17 Qd6 R×f5 18 Rg8+ Rf8 19 Q×f8 mate.

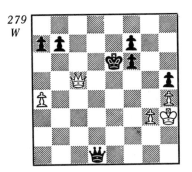

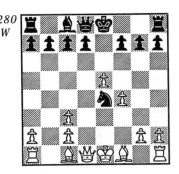

Chess Problems

The art of composing and solving set move positions, White to play and mate in x (usually 2 or 3) moves, is an interesting world of its own, having only minimum relations with the hurly-burly of the players' cut-throat world. These compositions are puzzles and yet they have more. One can admire their settings; and the way that ideas are blended and expressed within them. They are expected to conform to certain standards; there must be a use for every piece on the board; alternative solutions (cooks) are normally unacceptable; a key move giving check is grudgingly accepted only when the idea outweighs its execution.

The first position given (diag 281) was constructed by a famous 9th century composer, Abu'n Na'am, who was probably under the patronage of the Caliphs of Baghdad. Black is to move and win (actually to mate on his third move). The solutions runs **1 ... Nh4+ 2 R×h4 R×g3+ 3 K×g3 Re3** mate. It was characteristic of problems of that era for the losing side to be on the verge of an overwhelming win. Possibly money was wagered on the outcome of the position with the odds apparently stacked heavily in favour of the losing side.

There are four grandmasters for chess compositions recognised (in early 1974) by the Federation International des Echecs (FIDE). These include Comins Mansfield of England, who was born in 1896. Diagram 282, was published by *The Morning Post* (now incorporated with *The Daily Telegraph*) in 1923. White is to play and mate in two. If Black was to play,

White would have no difficulties—1 . . . d3 2 Qe7; 1 . . . Rg1 (or 3–8) 2 N1e2; 1 . . . Rh(or a–f)2 2 Ng3. But White has no good waiting move, his king moves allowing Black to check. In search for the solution one is tempted to look for knight mates in similar fashion, but it is the queen that mates after **1 Qa6**—threatening mates at e2 or g6 according to which way the black rook jumps; if 1 . . . d3 2 Qe6 mate.

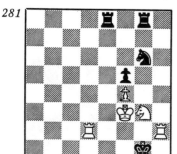

281

Black to play and win

282

White to play and mate in 2

Appendix 1 : Descriptive Notation

In descriptive notation, squares are named according to the number of the square along the file of the initial placing of the pieces, in abbreviated form. The squares are named from both the black and white side of the board, which means that each square has two names.

The initial square of White's queen is Queen 1 (abbreviated to Q1). Squares along the file from Q1 read Q2, Q3 . . . to Q8. The squares on the king file are described as K1, K2 . . . The black king, from White's point of view starts at K8, and from Black's point of view on K1.

The rook on the queen's side is regarded as the queen's rook (QR) and squares are labelled QR1, QR2. . . . The queen's knight (QN) and queen's bishop (QB) are treated similarly. The king-side pieces are prefixed by the letter K, e.g. KR, KN and KB.

The prefixes K and Q are dropped when there is no ambiguity, e.g. when the bishop on KB1 goes to QB4 (B–QB4) it can be written as B–B4 if the other bishop cannot go to KB4.

Captures are indicated by ×, e.g. B × N means bishop takes knight.

Other moves have a dash in the middle in place of 'to', e.g. P–K4, being pawn to king's fourth.

When it's necessary to distinguish between pieces in greater detail, one adds square on which the piece is, or will be placed, e.g. N/K5 × N/N6.

Descriptive notation is slowly becoming unfashionable. It is more cumbersome to use than the algebraic notation used throughout most of this book. The descriptive is considerably more expensive to print than the shortened algebraic.

For games using descriptive notation, see pp. 74, 74, 75, 78, 79, 79, 81 and 84.

Black

	a	b	c	d	e	f	g	h	
8	QR1/QR8	QN1/QN8	QB1/QB8	Q1/Q8	K1/K8	KB1/KB8	KN1/KN8	KR1/KR8	8
7	QR2/QR7	QN2/QN7	QB2/QB7	Q2/Q7	K2/K7	KB2/KB7	KN2/KN7	KR2/KR7	7
6	QR3/QR6	QN3/QN6	QB3/QB6	Q3/Q6	K3/K6	KB3/KB6	KN3/KN6	KR3/KR6	6
5	QR4/QR5	QN4/QN5	QB4/QB5	Q4/Q5	K4/K5	KB4/KB5	KN4/KN5	KR4/KR5	5
4	QR5/QR4	QN5/QN4	QB5/QB4	Q5/Q4	K5/K4	KB5/KB4	KN5/KN4	KR5/KR4	4
3	QR6/QR3	QN6/QN3	QB6/QB3	Q6/Q3	K6/K3	KB6/KB3	KN6/KN3	KR6/KR3	3
2	QR7/QR2	QN7/QN2	QB7/QB2	Q7/Q2	K7/K2	KB7/KB2	KN7/KN2	KR7/KR2	2
1	QR8/QR1	QN8/QN1	QB8/QB1	Q8/Q1	K8/K1	KB8/KB1	KN8/KN1	KR8/KR1	1
	a	b	c	d	e	f	g	h	

White

Appendix 2: Self-Assessment

(from p. 60)

Discussing your first reactions: they could be: 1 . . . Rb8— saving the rook; 1 . . . Bg4—counter-attacking on to White's queen; 1 . . . Bg4 intending 2 . . . Qd3 and 3 . . . Qe2 mate—attacking; 1 . . . Qd3 intending 2 . . . Bg4 and 3 . . . Qe2 mate—attacking; 1 . . . Qe7—very wild; 1 . . . N×e4 to approach the White king by . . . Qh4+ and/or . . . Bf2+—attacking; 1 . . . Ba6 intending 2 . . . Qd3—attacking.

Deep consideration could lead to one switching through all these possibilities. That would mean you have a wide ranging balanced approach to positions.

When calculated out Black's best is 1 . . . N×e4 and if 2 B×a8 Bf2+ 3 Ke2 Bg4+ wins the white queen, or 2 B×e4 Qh4+ and 3 . . . Q×e4, or 2 d4! Qf6 3 B×e4 Qh4+ 4 Kd2 Q×e4 with the white king a long-term target.

Bibliography.

The following books are particularly recommended or referred to in the text.

Encyclopedia of Chess Openings—ed. by A. Matanović (Batsford)

'Contemporary Chess Openings series' (Batsford):

 The Pirc Defence—G. S. Botterill, R. D. Keene

 The King's Indian Defence—L. Barden, W. R. Hartston and R. D. Keene

 The King's Gambit—V. Korchnoi and V. Zak

 Sicilian Dragon—D. N. L. Levy (Batsford)

 The Grünfeld Defence—W. R. Hartston (Batsford)

A History of Chess—H. J. R. Murray (Oxford)

Chess, East and West, Past and Present—The Metropolitan Museum of Art, New York

Chess Psychology—N. V. Krogius (Saratov, USSR)

'Computer Chess: Past, Present and Future'—David Levy (*Chess Life and Review*, Dec. 1973)

Think Like a Grandmaster—Alexander Kotov (Batsford)

Pawn Endings—Y. Averbakh, J. Maizelis (Batsford)

Rook Endings—V. Smyslov, G. Levenfish (Batsford)

The Games of Robert J. Fischer—ed. by R. G. Wade, K. J. O'Connell (Batsford)

200 Open Games—David Bronstein (Batsford)

The World Chess Championship—S. Gligoric, with all world championship games 1948–72 ed. by R. G. Wade (Batsford)

Index 1 : General

Index 2: Games and Positions (*white first*)

Index 3: People

Index 4 : Photographs and Sketches